Praise for **"G**

"This project challenges traditional methods of ministerial promotion through insightful and critical analysis. Current strategies are challenged and alternatives offered to those long-standing practices considered by many to be inequitable. Thank you Dr. GreeneBarr for having the courage to confront these issues."

Superintendant J. Drew Sheard, Senior Pastor
Greater Emmanuel Institutional Church of God in Christ
Detroit, MI

"It is an honor to recommend Dr. GreeneBarr's excellent book. This book moves beyond the usual focus on mentoring and takes the reader into the deeper realities and challenges of moving from calling to influential leadership. It was my privilege to observe the development of the book's foundational research. The reader will catch the spirit and passion of the author; and, this is the spirit of a true mentor."

Richard Leslie Parrott, Ph.D., President
President, Seize Your Life, Inc.
(Former Director of the Doctoral Program, Ashland Theological Seminary)

"Cecelia GreeneBarr provides us with a long-awaited model for mentoring clergy in the churches of the twenty-first century. She spells out in detail the need and promise of such mentoring and then takes us step-by-step through that process that leads from potential to transformation. This is a must-read for all leaders who find this task ennobling and take their mentoring responsibilities seriously. She includes a sermon on biblical leadership that is both thoughtful and provocative."

Cleophus J. LaRue, Ph.D
Associate Professor of Homiletics
Princeton Theological Seminary

"Dr. Greene-Barr's book, **Guide My Feet,** stands alone in its readable scholarly portrayal of Ministry Transformed through Mentoring. It is a must read for the church and academy in developing persons for transformed ministry. Persons who want to maximize their strengths and gifts while encouraging others to do the same will be greatly assisted by this book."

Reverend E. Anne Henning Byfield,
Presiding Elder
South District Indiana Conference,
African Methodist Episcopal Church

"I am so pleased to recommend this much needed work by Dr. Cecelia GreeneBarr. In the Black Church tradition the role of "Father and Mother in the ministry" has been very prevalent. Even though this relationship has been in place for generations, there has not been much in place to help those in the pastoral mentoring role to systematicly prepare these mentees for leadership. Dr. GreeneBarr's work is scholarly, yet practical. It is clear that she understands the church and the preacher. When you read and then apply the principles she so ably share I am sure you will join me in thanking her for this much needed work."

Bishop John R. Bryant, Presiding Bishop
Fifth Episcopal District
African Methodist Episcopal Church

"Mentoring has almost become a lost art, especially in ministry. We owe a debt of gratitude to Dr. GreeneBarr for her brilliance and scholarship on this much needed topic. I encourage every reader to both learn and enjoy the depth of knowledge shared in these pages. Both mentor and apprentice can gain support and direction from this dynamic work of art. Thanks Pastor Cecelia GreeneBarr! "

Reverend Edward L. Branch, Pastor
Third New Hope Baptist Church,
Detroit, MI

"Guide My Feet: Ministry Transformed Through Mentoring, is an important addition to the small body of published work on mentoring and how ministry can be shaped in this process. Reverend Dr. GreeneBarr has excelled in this academic and practical theological field and is to be commended for her scholarly yet readable approach. I highly recommend this work to my colleagues in ministry and their students."

Reverend Albert D. Tyson, III, Pastor
St. Stephen African Methodist Episcopal Church
Chicago, IL

"I am pleased to endorse my colleague, Dr. Cecelia GreeneBarr's literary work *Guide My Feet: Ministry Transformed Through Mentoring*. We live in a parentless generation. People are seeking genuine, sincere, caring and concerned people to mentor, coach and guide them through life's many transitions. Indeed, her focus on the foundation for the future and guidance for godliness and the legacy of leadership will prove to be a catalyst for growth for all who read this book.

I commend her, congratulate her and stand with her in faith. Get your Bible studies together, use it as a guide, personal devotion or study, you will be blessed."

Bishop Donald Hilliard, Jr., Senior Pastor
Cathedral International
Perth Amboy, NJ

Rev. Dr. Cecelia GreeneBarr

guide my feet

Ministry Transformed Through Mentoring

Foreword by Rev. Dr. William Watley

GreeneHouse, LLC • Walled Lake, Michigan

Guide My Feet
Ministry Transformed Through Mentoring

For information, contact
GreeneHouse, LLC
P.O. Box 714 • Walled Lake, MI 48390
www.greenehousellc.com

ISBN: (10) 9796366-0-4
ISBN: (13) 978-0-9796366-0-8

Library of Congress Catalog No. 2007931134

Cover and Interior Design by Selah Branding & Design
www.selahbrandinganddesign.com

Printed in the United States of America

Dedication

My husband, Theron E. Barr, Jr.
whose enduring friendship, confidence, support and
love has served as a light of hope in my life's journey.
You never let me forget that this book was still
sitting on the shelf, waiting for God's open door.

and

My toddlers; Cecelia and Theron-Howard;
Through your eyes, smiles and consuming
love I can see the favor of God.

and

My pastoral appointment;
Trinity African Methodist Episcopal Church,
the incubator for my spiritual energy.

and

My teacher, friend and mentor beloved,
the late Rev. Dr. Samuel DeWitt Proctor.

ACKNOWLEDGMENTS

The first time I wrote the acknowledgments for my Doctor of Ministry dissertation that has now become this published literary work, I was excited and grateful to those who helped me along the way. My heart is still overflowing with thanks. It is not possible to name everyone who provided inspiration for the completion of this work, but expressions are presented to the following people;

To my husband, **Theron Barr, Jr.,** thank you for your flexibility in necessary adjustments that make ministry possible. I appreciate your love and commitment to our children, home and overall well-being.

To my children, **Cecelia and Theron-Howard Barr,** Mommy loves you and always gets joy when you affirm my place in your life by saying, "You are the best mommy in the whole world!"

To my mother, **Loretta Greene,** thank you for coming to Michigan an entire year to help with the children.

To my cousin, **Alfreda Loatman**, thank you for fasting with me, discerning the move of God with me and being with me everyday of this project.

To those clergy leaders who have been the voice of wisdom for me along this pastoral journey; **Rev. Leon G. Lipscombe, Rev. Albert D. Tyson III, Rev. William D. Watley, Ph.D.**

Bishop Millicent Hunter and Presiding Elder Anne Henning Byfield. I'm glad that you always answer the phone.

LaTanya Orr, CEO of Selah Branding and Design, thank you for the seed into my ministry. Without you hearing and submitting to the voice of God, this work would still be sitting on the shelf. Your gift will make room for you.

Trinity AME Church, thank you for receiving me as your pastor. These three years have established fertile spiritual ground for all of us.

Finally, I honor God for making this happen. The Lord really does know the plans He has for us. Every dream, vision and prophetic word has come to pass. Praises be to the Lord.

Rev. Dr. Cecelia E. GreeneBarr
Founder, Sharing Faith Ministries
President, GreeneHouse, LLC

PREFACE

GUIDE MY FEET
A Traditional Negro Spiritual

Guide my feet, while I run this race
Guide my feet, while I run this race
Guide my feet while I run this race, for
I don't want to run this race in vain!

Hold my hand...
Stand by me...
I'm your child...

Search my heart, while I run this race
Search my heart, while I run this race
Search my heart, while I run this race, for
I don't want to run this race in vain!

This Negro Spiritual speaks to the desire for divine direction into a new reality. Likewise the content of this book has been crafted as part of that guidance into a new reality. There are limitations in that questions still remain and solutions still need to be unearthed but it does hold the reader's hand, it keeps the reader from feeling like she/he is standing alone, and it certainly causes the reader to search their own heart while they run this race of ministry.

The work you are about to read was compiled for my Doctor of Ministry degree which I earned October 2002. It was then entitled: *Mentoring – The Critical Link in Clergy Development: Effective Practices of Identifying, Mentoring and Elevating Clergy Apprentices for Leadership*. Prayerfully I have taken research and made it palatable for the practical consumer.

The research and development has certainly been a prayerful journey. Even with the publication of this book, the journey is only just beginning. The next step is actualizing every aspect of the model. Believer, after reading this book you may ask yourself what next? Permit me to suggest that your next steps be towards intentional participation in the Mentoring Model.

Modeling the Kingdom of God,
Rev. Dr. Cecelia E. GreeneBarr

TABLE OF CONTENTS

FOREWORD

Robin had Batman. Aqua lad had Aqua man. In the Star Wars Epic, Anakin Skywalker had the Dark Lord of the Sith, Obie Wan Kenobi had Qui-Gon Jinn, and Luke Skywalker had Obie Wan Kenobi. Joshua had Moses. Elisha had Elijah. Ruth had Naomi. The disciples had Jesus. Timothy had Paul.

Whether the context is secular or sacred, corporate or church, financial or family, profit or non-profit, mentoring is critical for the successful continuation of any cause, movement, institution, organization or family. Yet as vital and as fundamental as mentoring is, it is sometimes one of the most neglected aspects of dynamic visionaries, growing organizations and well established institutions. Many times churches, movements, and other kinds of organizations that start out spreading like wild fire, fizzle into a spark or fade into oblivion with the passing away of a founding personality or generation, because the issues of succession and mentoring have not been thought out or planned. Sometimes growth was so rapid and the challenges of rapid growth were so many that those who were responsible for planning for the future never got around to it.

Sometimes organizations and movements operate under the unrealistic assumption that certain leaders will always be around to give guidance and furnish the necessary charismatic leadership and problem solving capability in times of crisis. Sometimes powerful leadership is afraid to grapple with the issue of its own mortality and how does one address the inevitable "institutionalization of charisma" that comes with the passing of time. Whatever the reason or reasons, a system of mentoring that has not been put into place painfully results in movements, organizations, churches, companies, and families that were once considered cutting edge but have now been cut down to only a remnant of the dynamism, strength, viability and respectability they once had.

Those who shop for groceries as well as those who use medicine, are familiar with the concept of shelf life. When a consumable item is placed on a shelf, sometimes words are printed on that item that tell us that the particular food, drink or medicine are best used by a certain date. That expiration date defines its shelf life. No matter what the consumable food, drink or medicine is, no matter who the manufacturer is, no matter how much the item cost, no matter how up to date the technology in terms of its preparation, every perishable item has a certain shelf life, after which neither the store nor the manufacturer will guarantee its freshness, its taste or effectiveness. No manufacturer would assume that its product has unlimited and eternal shelf life regarding quality. Even these human bodies have limited shelf life. The word of God tells us, "The days of our lives are seventy years, or perhaps eighty, if we are strong; even then their span is only toil and trouble; they are soon gone, and we fly away" (Psalm 90: 10 NRSV).

As common as the reality of shelf life is, there are any number of ministries and movements, organizations and causes, families and institutions which function as if shelf life does not apply to them. Many such entities behave as if their dynamism, relevance, power and prominence are self sustaining throughout ceaseless ages. Many such entities take the words of Matthew 6: 34 out of context and too literally, when the Lord said, "So do not worry about tomorrow, for tomorrow will bring worries of its own. Today's trouble is enough for today." When such entities fail to make provision for their future by mentoring those who will pick up the mantles that former generations have carried but must now release, those entities are soon regarded as historic anachronisms whose significance is found in a bygone era, but are out of touch with both the tenor of the times and their ongoing market. Such entities are soon replaced by those whose message and style fit the market and audience that needs to be reached. Mentoring addresses the issue of continued, effective and relevant shelf life for both message and mission for anything or anyone who see themselves as being intergenerational and multidimensional.

Mentoring then, requires that leadership understand that true vision must extend beyond itself. Sometimes leadership only sees itself as making a contribution to one generation and for one generation, primarily its own. II Kings 20 and Isaiah 39 tells about an incident that occurred in the latter days of the reign of King Hezekiah. Hezekiah was one of the kings who sought the Lord's face and who sought to govern the people of God according to the word and will of God. According to the scriptures, Hezekiah received a visit from the Babylonian king Merodach-baladan of Babylon. Hezekiah graciously welcomed his guests. Hezekiah "showed them all his treasure house, the silver, the gold, the spices, the precious oil, his armory, all that was found in his storehouses; there was nothing in his house or in all his realm that Hezekiah did not show them."

The prophet Isaiah approached Hezekiah and asked who his guests were and where they came from. Hezekiah told the prophet that they had come from the far country of Babylon, and when Isaiah asked him what he had shown them in his house, Hezekiah replied, "They have seen all that is in my house; there is nothing in my storehouses that I did not show them." Then Isaiah told Hezekiah, "Hear the word of the Lord: Days are coming when all that is in your house, and that which your ancestors have stored up until this day, shall be carried to Babylon; nothing shall be left, says the Lord. Some of your own sons who are born to you shall be taken away; they shall be eunuchs in the palace of the king of Babylon." What was Hezekiah's response to this word from Isaiah? Hezekiah said, "The word of the Lord that you have spoken is good." For he thought, 'There will be peace and security in my days.'" The word of God went on to say, "Hezekiah slept with his ancestors; and his son Manasseh succeeded him." As much as Hezekiah accomplished and as powerful as his prayers were, he only had vision for peace and security in his day. His son Manasseh who succeeded him started off being one of the worst kings of Israel whose reign was totally opposite in character to that of his father. The result was that the prophecy delivered by Isaiah came to pass and Manasseh did spend time in chains in Babylon.

Such is the high cost of a failure to have vision beyond one's own time and such is the tragedy of failing to mentor those who will have the responsibility of leadership in times to come.

Mentoring can only take place in an atmosphere and context when leadership is secure. Insecure leadership cannot mentor properly. A casual look at the relationship between Saul and David is the classic case study of a mentoring relationship that went bad because of the insecurity of the mentor. David came into Saul's life to be a blessing to him. The relationship was going well until after a certain victory David had won against the Philistines, who were an ancient people that were often at odds with the Israelites. When David returned from his victory over the Philistines, "the women came out of the towns of Israel, singing and dancing, to meet King Saul, with tambourines, with songs of joy, and with musical instruments. And the women sang to one another as they made merry, 'Saul has killed his thousands, and David his ten thousands.'" The word of God tells us that, "Saul was very angry, for this saying displeased him. He said, 'They have ascribed to David ten thousands, and to me they have ascribed thousands; what more can he have but the kingdom?' So Saul eyed David from that day on." The very next day as David played his lyre for Saul, a jealous and jaundiced Saul attempted to kill David with his spear, but David eluded him twice (I Samuel 18: 6-11). Saul eventually chased David, a bright, young, talented and anointed warrior, who had the favor of God upon him, away from his presence. Saul lost the talents, gifts, friendship and assistance of a young man who could have added so very much to his reign. Such is the tragedy of insecure leadership that has no vision beyond itself. Mentoring takes place when leadership has a vision for a future beyond itself and when it is secure.

Contrast the examples of King Hezekiah and King Saul with that of the Lord Jesus Christ who mentored twelve apostles to carry on the movement he started after his ascension. Note his words of empowerment to them, "Very truly, I tell you, the one who believes in me will also do the works that I do and, in fact, will do greater works than these, because I am going to the Father (John 14: 13, NRSV). The Christian faith as we know it, that has turned the world upside down and right side up is not only due to the life, death, resurrection, ascension and continuing ministry of intercession and promised return of the Lord Jesus. The Christian faith as we have come to know, believe and follow it is also due to the fact that the Lord Jesus poured so much of himself into the apostles he mentored. Since the Lord did not write anything down while he was here on earth, whatever we know about him came from the life and witness of the apostles he mentored and those that the apostles mentored. Such is the triumph and glorious ongoing power of an organization, movement or kingdom when mentoring is done correctly by leadership that is secure and has a vision beyond itself.

Of course any relationship, including a mentoring relationship is a two way street. There must not only be a willingness of mentors to give, there must also be receptivity from those who are recipients of the mentors' instructions and guidance to receive. My own experience has shown me that the lack has not been on the side of those who are willing to receive, but on the part of those who are prepared to mentor. When one looks at the vital importance of mentoring, the need for mentors and the hunger of those who are looking for mentors, this book by Dr. Greene Barr addresses a major issue, not only in the Kingdom, but in leadership development in general. My hope and prayer is that the insights gained from her studies and experience will help guide the feet of those who seek to exercise leadership and to have ministries that are truly transformational.

Rev. Dr. William D. Watley,

INTRODUCTION

The purpose and focus of this project was to develop a model for professional clergy to identify, mentor and elevate women and men through a clergy apprenticeship and into transformational leadership. The critical question was: What is an effective process for professional clergy to methodically and intentionally identify, mentor and elevate clergy apprentices into transformational leadership?

This model emerged from analyzing the trials and errors of clergy leaders and their apprentices who have lived the process of call identification, mentoring and elevation. It resulted in strategies designed to raise levels of consciousness concerning clergy apprenticeship. Through the implementation of the model, the ministerial community in general, mentors and their apprentices will be exposed to biblical teaching, forum discussions, creative learning and supportive structures designed to enhance the intentional practices of mentoring. Each strategic unit of the model uniquely targets a particular population within the ministerial community.

During the formation of this project, the model was mentally conceived as one cohesive approach that would address each of the six goals. The first goal was for the model to help professional clergy leaders identify God's calling upon clergy apprentices. The second goal was for the model to help professional clergy leaders implement methods to mentor clergy apprentices. The model would help professional clergy leaders discern when it is time to elevate their clergy apprentice into leadership. The model would persuade professional clergy leaders to value and participate in a mentoring/apprentice process. The model would help professional clergy leaders accept their responsibility in the training of their ministerial staff. Recognizing that the mentoring experience often crosses the official lines of ministerial staffs, goal number five emphasizes the need for official staff members to become involved in intentional mentoring, whereas goal number four removes any official boundaries. And the final goal was for the model to be based in the mentor/teacher training modeled by Jesus (see Chapter 3). Research steered the project design away from one cohesive approach and towards a multifaceted strategy in order to address each of the project goals.

The Mentoring Model was reviewed by a panel of 24 professional clergy, followed by an opportunity for the panel member to ask questions if additional clarity was necessary. Once the panel member was clear about the structure of the model, they were asked to assess each of the goals.

Two groups of professional clergy leaders were interviewed for this project — persons who are theologically informed and reflective. The first group represented mentors who have, by reputation, demonstrated an intentional act of developing clergy into transformational leaders. The second group represented clergy leaders who previously served as an apprentice to a member of the first group. In a couple of exceptions where the apprentices were unavailable, the information from the mentor was still included. Both groups, mentors and apprentices, received a list of questions. Specifically, mentors were asked to share their systems of identifying the potential of clergy apprentices, tactics for developing the apprentice's dormant giftedness and strategies used to elevate the apprentice into transformational leadership. Some of the mentors' responses were generalized reflections that collectively represented former apprentices. Apprentices were interviewed as a balance group and judged to see if they received the principles, insight and wisdom, their mentor believed they had instilled. Based on the information obtained, a model was designed, with a goal of publication as an informed resource for professional clergy to use as a guidepost in their ministerial work of apprenticing clergy into transformational leaders.

This project is connected to my personal experiences in ministry. I am an African American woman, who spent her formative years in the Baptist church, and ministry years in the African Methodist Episcopal Church. Two years after earning a Master of Divinity degree from Princeton Theological Seminary, I was ordained an itinerant elder. While I awaited denominational leadership to discern my giftedness for ministry and to elevate me into service as a pastor, in 1999 I established a Christ-centered ministry entitled Sharing Faith Ministries (SFM) that is independent from my participation in the African Methodist Episcopal Church (AMEC). It is through SFM that the model created from my research will be implemented.

Many of my experiences in ministry have been

wrought with mismanagement, indifference, and intentional misdirection from some clergy who exercised direct pastoral authority, and other clergy who had indirect power over my ministerial development. The consequences on my behalf have been disillusionment, frustration, attacks upon my confidence and a deep yearning for a more excellent way. In an answer to prayer, God established a relationship between a veteran clergy mentor and myself that provided meaningful direction for the path I am now traveling as a minister. During those times when I felt the most defeated, my mentor was the avenue God used to help me spiritually and emotionally manage the events of my past. The project seeks to honor the memory of my first mentor; Rev. Dr. Samuel DeWitt Proctor, and subsequent mentors, while at the same time transforming my energy and experiences into a resource that will positively help other clergy.

SIGNIFICANT TERMS

Clergy Leader: An ordained minister who exemplifies exceptional emotional intelligence (Goleman 1998), scholarly preparation to include the area of theology, and leadership competencies for ministry (Berlinger 1998). The location of their ministry may include the traditional congregational setting, social justice ministries, para-church organizations, chaplaincy, or theological education.

Clergy Apprentice: A layperson who has yet to accept God's call to ministry, as well as a minister who has yet to recognize the depth of God's call upon their life. God anoints such persons for ministry but their gifts, both spiritual and innate talents, remain stagnant or underutilized. A relationship of supervised leadership development with a clergy leader may have already been established. Such a relationship serves as an incubator of consistency and coherence (Proctor 1989, p. 27) where spiritual gifts and talents are heightened and vision for ministry is expanded. The goal for the clergy apprentice extends beyond the rite of passage known as ordination and prepares them for exceptional service as a transformational leader.

Congregation: Location of ministry extends beyond traditional worship centers, and includes chaplain assignments or para-church ministries.

Elevate: Marks the completion of the apprentice training and the beginning of the actualization of ministry calling. This is a transitional closure where the clergy leader shifts roles to include becoming a professional colleague to their apprentice. This transition requires the clergy leader to use their personal influence and professional contacts in securing a new leadership position to be fulfilled by the former apprentice. The clergy leader also positions the community to recognize the new status of the former apprentice.

Identify: Discerning a divine mandate (Nore'n 1992, p. 15) for ministry upon the life of a clergy apprentice.

Mentor: The clergy leader who has mastery over the performance and ministry skills being transmitted (Milavec 1982, p. 85) and transfers them for the purpose of empowering the clergy apprentice to perform likewise in their area of calling. Additional qualities as defined by Clinton are as follows: mentors must be able to see potential in a person; they can tolerate mistakes in order to see potential develop; they are flexible and patient; they have vision and are able to suggest next steps in the apprentice's development; they also demonstrate the spiritual gifts of mercy, giving, exhortation, faith and word of wisdom. The mentor is a clergy leader who helps the apprentice by; giving timely advice, risking their own reputation, models and sets expectations that challenge, provides literary information, gives financially, sometimes sacrificially, to further the apprentice's ministry, co-ministers in order to increase the credibility, status and prestige of the apprentice and promotes the apprentice beyond the mentor's own level of leadership (Clinton 1988, p. 130). Mentors are attentive to both the operational activities and spiritual formation of their apprentice. Mentors seek to facilitate balanced growth among apprentices to include leadership, character and skills development.

Professional Clergy: An ordained minister, who has invested in their ministry through academic preparation, participation with clergy associations, adheres to a code of ethics and submits him or herself to a forum of accountability.

Spiritual Apprenticeship: For the purpose of this project, our definition includes six characteristics provided by Anderson and Reese. These characteristics are:

- The quality of being relational between mentor and apprentice.
- Opportunity available to be autobiographical by both mentors and apprentice.
- Partnership with the Holy Spirit.
- Spiritual Apprenticeship is purposive.
- Spiritual Apprenticeship requires listening.
- Spiritual Apprenticeship requires adaptable discernment (Anderson and Reese 1999, pp. 37-55).

Theologically Informed: The clergy leader has earned a scholarly degree in the discipline of theology from an accredited seminary. The clergy leader's education has also been supplemented by continuing theological education and independent study.

Transformational Leadership: An above-average ability to influence visionary and transformational change beyond ones own immediate domain. This process of change influences men and women toward God's purposes for the group (Clinton 1988, p. 14). As defined by Herrington, Bonem and Furr, transformational leadership is influence that helps followers embrace a vision of the preferred future. Transformational leaders inspire and empower followers to achieve new levels of personal and corporate performance. They encourage individuals and support innovative ventures. Leaders expand their involvement beyond the managerial role of planning and implementing programs and events. In this study, transformational leadership is a functional quality and activity that is not the same as being a manager. Common characteristics of a transformational leader include change, continuous learning, interdependence, risk and ambiguity (2000, p. 96).

CHAPTER 1

A Legacy Of Leadership

As you think about mentors (these individuals) and the determinative impact they have had, you can quickly see why relationships with mentors are not an option for people (men) today, but an essential. Mentors look inside us and find the person (man) we long to be. Then they help to bring that person (man) to life. At their best, mentors nurture our souls. They shape our character. They call us to become complete (men), whole (men), and, by the grace of God, holy (men)

(Howard and William Hendricks 1995, p. 18).

> But never forget that the agenda you bring [to
> a mentoring relationship] is always the tip
> of the iceberg. There are always underlying
> issues — especially issues of character. (And)
> That's the value of mentoring. It starts with
> the things you want to work on, and ideally
> leads to the things you need to work on
>
> (Howard and William Hendricks 1995, p. 102).

An Ingredient for Success

In 1993, *Ebony* magazine began to periodically conduct a poll among the "Ebony's 100+ Most Influential Black Americans" (*Ebony* 1993, p. 156), in an attempt to recognize African American pastors and preachers, and to classify 15 as America's Greatest Black Preachers" (*Ebony* 1993, p. 156). Curious and competitive readers were left to speculate about the ingredient of the honorees' ministerial reputation and success. Whereas success is a relative term, and it is not the goal of this project to generate fame, the underlying message was that some leaders are more capable and effectual than others.

Not surprising, but the 1993 poll did not include any female clergy, although a few women did receive notable mention. Perhaps this absence is what prompted *Ebony* magazine in 1997, to conduct a similar comparison, restricted to female clergy, in which the same methodology resulted in the "Fifteen Greatest Female Preachers" (Kinnon 1997, p. 102). On a base level, these rating articles brought to the forefront, a sense of professional competition and celebrity appeal present within the clergy community. I began to suspect that their ministerial reputations and success in ministry had a common ingredient, in the form of a mentor, someplace along the path of their development. My suspicions were further affirmed as I have observed the progress of younger and even inexperienced clergy moving into opportunities made available to them largely due to the influence of their mentors.

Unexplored Leadership Potential

Mentoring, in general terms, has become a very popular concept for volunteers who work with youth and even corporate training, but in the church it is something very different. In the church, clergy will espouse the benefits that mentoring relationships provide, but unearthing those who will avail themselves to the work of methodical and intentional mentoring of other clergy is a mammoth task. For every chronicled success in ministry, such as the *Ebony* magazine polls, there is a pool of less hopefuls who never come within reach of their Godly appointments. Unfortunately, the ministry of the Kingdom suffers because there are scores of persons who never even receive an opportunity to serve in ministry on the level of their calling.

Unfortunately, the ministry of the Kingdom suffers because there are scores of persons who never even receive an opportunity to serve in ministry on the level of their calling.

Gospel recording artist Miami Mass Choir produced a popular song entitled, "What God Has For Me" (Miami Mass Choir 2001) that so often sounds like a personal mantra for those seeking their divine destiny in the Kingdom of God. The song boldly affirms that God's blessings for us, as individuals, will be realized. But as Myles Monroe critically summaries in the introduction of *Understanding Your Potential,* God has created each person with divine purpose, but for a number of reasons, some people never participate in the manifestation of their potential.

> Though it may surprise you, the riches deposits on our planet lie just a few blocks from your house. They rest in your local cemetery or graveyard. Buried beneath the soil within the walls of those sacred grounds are dreams that never came to pass, songs that were never sung, books that were never written, paintings that never filled a canvas, ideas that were never shared, visions that never became reality, inventions that were never designed, plans that never went beyond the drawing board of the mind and purposes that were never fulfilled. Our graveyards are filled with potential that remained potential. What a tragedy! (Monroe 1991, p. 6).

I am deeply concerned with occurrences, wherein divinely called persons do not reach their potential in Kingdom leadership, due to a lack of effective mentoring or the unfortunate cases of pastoral mismanagement, experienced along any phase of call identification, mentoring and leadership elevation. Giftedness, as a singular quality does not account for why some have exceptional results and peer recognition, while others do not. Nor does a lack of giftedness hinder some from receiving positions. Methodically and intentionally mentoring women and men through a clergy apprenticeship helps the apprentice to realize their individual potential and the impact that their potential can have on the Kingdom of God.

Leading, But Not Called —Called, But Not Leading

Leadership in the Kingdom of God will always be subject to the infiltration of persons who have made an academic decision to choose ministry as a career (Oden 1983, pp. 8-20). In my observation, these persons are skilled in camouflaging their lack of divine call, gifting and anointing of the Holy Spirit and have been unleashed on unsuspecting congregations. The peril is that these ministers mimic the outward signs of leadership or charisma, while many authentically called persons flounder in their calling due to the absence of competent mentoring along the three incubational modules of leadership development as described in this project. For some, this absence has resulted in abandonment of pursuing God's calling on and purpose in their lives. While the development of this model won't eliminate contamination among Kingdom leadership, it is hoped that its implementation will yield quality clergy leaders who are posed and positioned into transformational leadership.

Giftedness, as a singular quality does not account for why some have exceptional results and peer recognition, while others do not.

Leading Out of Position

Another type who has been unleashed upon congregations is a clergy person with an authentic call but who functions outside the area of their calling or giftedness. Where some denominations primarily affirm (ordain) one form of ministry, such as the pastorate, it creates environments where clergy apprentices are hedged into ministries even though their calling and skills clearly point towards other areas. In the end, denominations and congregations suffer, clergy apprentices may become damaged and their full participation in the Kingdom of God is delayed, and, in extreme scenarios, aborted.

A mentoring model is needed that is accommodating to the diverse and creative roles of leadership that God chooses. A mentoring model is needed that supports the uniqueness of the apprentice and encourages an authentic response to the call that God has placed upon their life. This authentic response becomes grounded by integrity to the inner witness of the Holy Spirit and a supportive system of clergy leaders.

Positioned for Advancement

A phenomenon is spreading in the ministerial community, it is called by several names; adjutant and armor bearer (1 Samuel 16:21) are the most common, but the purpose is consistent. These individuals or ministers-in-waiting, perform duties of service to their clergy leader under the heading of submitting to authority, acts of humility, willingness to serve and because it gains them access to an otherwise inaccessible leader. The dilemma of this phenomenon is the misconception on behalf of the leader that this level of interaction qualifies as mentoring. The intent evaporates, therefore causing the mentor to conclude that presence, alone, qualifies as mentoring. Missing qualities in this environment are two-way commitment, equal professional esteem and a relationship grounded in mutuality.

Beyond Ordination

Denominations and the governing bodies for nondenominational churches all have a procedure for preparing candidates to enter ordained ministry. The typical procedure usually involves completion of some level of theological studies, active participation in the ministry of the local church and examination before a board of established ministers. Although this process is potentially rigorous, and it can produce ordained clergy, it does not automatically facilitate the spiritual, emotional and practical qualities of transformational leadership. A new pattern such as the model designed in this project, is needed to supplement the ordination process.

Discerning the call to ministry in ones own life is at the very least inexact and mystical. Embracing that call and moving on into practical ministry, isolated from experienced counsel, is dangerous for the clergy apprentice and their future ministries. Competent clergy leaders do not simply appear on the scene as out of a puff of smoke. Their presence and leadership skills development requires an incubation process (Proctor 1989, p. 21) followed by an inauguration of elevation in order for the experience to be meaningful to the apprentice and constructive for the Kingdom of God. Therefore, this project seeks to methodically and intentionally determine a necessary incubation process for the authentically called out persons to be positioned for success as clergy leaders in the Kingdom of God.

Issues of Gender, Denomination and Ethnicity

My experience as a woman shaped my reflections and sensitized the level of listening that I engaged during the research, but it did not cause me to develop a model specially designed towards the needs of female clergy. My aim was to develop a gender-neutral model. I certainly am aware and recognize that peculiarities exist when the apprenticeship involves both genders.

Mentoring is a time-consuming endeavor and when a clergy leader makes the conscious decision to intentionally enter into this relationship, the mentor is more prone to reinvest himself or herself in someone of like gender. It's just natural to seek the path of least resistance. This resistance appears under various manifestations of sexism in the church. The difference here, however, is that God does not exercise discrimination against women in any role of Kingdom participation, including leadership.

A woman's burden in following Jesus, as leader, is something that only a woman can intimately understand. Resistance is ever present, though subtle in form. Even qualities that are otherwise revered in a woman become a burden for clergy. I have observed, and it was communicated during the research interviews, that, in general, men find it more complicated to mentor women. Complications dramatically increase when the woman (either mentor or apprentice) is considered beautiful or attractive. The complications are indicative of false accusations, rumors, jealousy, insecurity and other devices used to malign either person's character.

Another complication that affects the female-male relationship during mentoring is the difference in each gender's communication style. Recognizing that each style is valuable, the differences make it possible for misunderstandings and inappropriate reactions to surface.

The occurrences of limited vision may also infest the female-male mentoring process, especially at the point of elevation. Culturally and socially tainted male mentors may find themselves imposing a limited vision onto their female apprentice. Conversely, in an environment where religious politics controls the process of elevation, males may discount females as potential mentors because they assume that females have less or limited influence within the larger denominational structure, thus not being able to broker the ideal leadership placement. These are just a few of the peculiarities that exist when the apprenticeship involves both genders. My experience as a female clergy does not ignore these peculiarities, but I do acknowledge the potential of this subject as the focus of an independent research project.

By the same token, my experience as an African American in the African Methodist Episcopal Church also shaped my reflections and sensitized my level of listening during the research, but it did not cause me to develop a model specifically designed towards the needs of the Black church, the AMEC or the African American community. My aim was to develop a model that escaped the boundaries of denominational, cultural and ethnic walls. The emphasis in this project is the Kingdom of God, not the limitations of humanity. I certainly am aware and recognize the racial divide among Christians, but I do so acknowledging the potential of that subject as the focus of an independent research project.

A Comprehensive Apprenticeship

This model was designed to methodically and intentionally develop transformational leaders in the Kingdom of God. There are three modules that comprise a comprehensive apprenticeship. The first is the process of identifying the call of God upon the life of women and men. The call identification may be acknowledged by the mentor or by the individual. Such identification positions them to become a clergy apprentice. The second includes the activities of a spiritual apprenticeship in the form of mentoring between the apprentice and the mentor. The final module is the elevation into leadership positions. As independent units, each one has significant influence upon the developing leader, but when united by a meaningful transition from one module to the next, the entire process gains depth and dimension.

Our model includes four strategies for disseminating knowledge, inspiring participation and facilitating learning. The primary objective is to lead from the heart, wherein the preacher's life experiences become a vibrant part of the model. The flexibility of each strategy shares the spirit of Howard Thurman's testimony as he reflected on methods of learning and development. "I believe that above all else the preacher's life experiences, with his successes and failures, hopes and aspirations, make up the only authentic laboratory in which all his fundamental commitments can be tested" (Thurman 1979, p. 161).

Each strategic unit is targeted for a unique segment population. The Intensive Training Unit will be a one-year creative learning incubator that meets quarterly for one week. Targeted participants are sets of mentors and their apprentices. Peer Mentoring Unit will be clergy who desire to collaborate with other clergy, for the accomplishment of their individual ministries. The Conference Unit will be a partnership with established ministries that presently conduct leadership conferences for clergy. Presentation of ideas will be a catalyst to awaken the mentor hidden within. Participants in the Conference Unit are progressive clergy interested in professional development. The Broadcast Unit will be a weekly radio talk forum where mentors share general wisdom concerning ministry and their experience of being mentored. Audiences consist of men and women who do not have mentors yet still need access to the wisdom that mentors are willing to share.

CHAPTER 2

The Call To Leadership

*Then I heard the voice of the Lord saying, "Whom
shall I send, and who will go for us?" And I said,
"Here am I; send me!" And he said, "Go and say
to this people…" (Isaiah 6:8-9).*

In the African American community of faith, we have
become accustomed to hearing about the sundry ways
that God uses to commission Christians into ministry.
Regardless to your denominational affiliation or ethnic
heritage, people are affected differently when they hear the
voice of the Lord, especially when they are not expecting to
hear God speak to them personally and directly as Isaiah

heard in the sixth chapter. There can be self-doubting about whether or not it was God who just spoke or if it were a mulling generated from their own hearts desire. Imagine the surprise by those who are predisposed to doubt that God still speaks and commissions followers to dedicate their lives for the service of the cross. For those about to participate in the Kingdom of God as a transformed leader, the ability to hear God is a non-negotiable that must be guarded. We who have been chosen by God to serve His church must be able to hear the voice of the Lord at the onset of our leadership journey and we need to discipline ourselves to keep our ear to the ground for any shifting that God is making in

our callings after our journey has begun.

For those about to participate in the Kingdom of God as a transformed leader, the ability to hear God is a non-negotiable that must be guarded.

Discerning the call to ministry in one's own life is at the very least inexact and mystical because over time, assignments from God have a tendency to morph. The location of ministry may change, the intensity of your approach may lessen or enhance. A ministry assignment that began as the foundation of a para-church organization to meet a need in your neighborhood may morph into a global initiative. Hearing the voice of the Lord and discerning the intention of God's heart each step of the way is non-negotiable for transformed clergy leaders for these very reasons.

We tell our call stories as a way of relieving inner pressure and as a way of continuing to understand the spiritual process of disclosure. When telling our call stories the mystery of the call produces intrigue in the listener while at the same time it may be exasperating for the subject of God's attention. William Myers is one who has observed the mystery of God's call, "I have listened to many stories from students who were wrestling with their call to preach, and I attempted to give them some direction, particularly African American students" (Myers 1992, p. xiv).

I am not seeking to prove that the "call" is a valid Christian experience. I unapologetically affirm the call as a valid Christian experience and I do so in solid theological company. Theologians and Christian scholars have written extensively on the origin and nature of God's call. In *Faith Seeking Understanding*, Daniel Migliore describes the call to Christian ministry.

> But there is also a narrower meaning of the term Christian ministry. Among the diverse gifts of the Spirit to the church is the calling and ordination of certain people to the ministry of Word and sacrament. Ministry in this sense is an office that is ordained by God to provide for regular and responsible preaching of the gospel, celebration of the sacraments, and leadership in the life and service of the church ... The call to the ministry of Word and sacrament has both an inward and an outward aspect. People are called to this ministry by the Holy Spirit, who bestows special gifts and motivates their recipients to dedicate their lives to the gospel ministry (Migliore 1991, p. 227).

My work departs from a position that the "call" to ministry is dynamic in origin and perpetually divine. Julia

Brogdon's call narrative is one of several in a collection edited by William Myers. Her story is an example of a personal reality interpreted through the lens of a biblical experience.

> I think that part of me has always known that I had a calling without really being able to clarify that … In elementary school one day, all of a sudden, just seemingly out of nowhere, I began to sense the presence of God. I began to feel with my spirit. I know now that there were questions being raised with me in regard to my future. I didn't know at that time how to reply to the questions that were being raised within me, but I knew that it meant, again for me, that God had a special work for me to do … When I was sixteen years old …while I was lying there to be stitched up, (after a near fatal car accident) that I heard a voice, wherein the Lord said to me, asked me — like a Damascus Road experience — the Lord said, "You know that you have work to do for me." I said, lying there with the doctor stitching me up, "I'll go." Just those two words, "I'll go. " It was in saying "I'll go" as I laid there, that there was a tremendous peace that came over me
> (Myers 1992, pp. 51-53).

"… Here Am I …"

Isaiah embraced God's call to leadership without coercion, cajoling or the persuading tactics many of us needed to give God our yes answer. Now, I say this knowing full well that having a seraph touch your mouth with a live coal might qualify as a significant act of persuasion. Truth is, even after one has heard the voice of the Lord, they may still need help to embrace how that call should be lived in the context of the community assignment. For example, take a leader who has lived all of their life in an urban area, earned their theological education in an urban area but God's plan for their ministry is in a rural factory town. It is easy to see how one might find it difficult to embrace the assignment in a manner authentic to the context.

Lest we forget there is the socio-political component of Kingdom leadership that also begs to be embraced. Depending on your interpretation of the relationship between church and state, you may believe that it is the church's responsibility to speak for the disenfranchised. You may also believe that someone should take a stand against systemic evil. But if your background has been shaped by passive resistance or complete non-involvement you may not be able to see yourself being used of God in such a confrontational manner. Yet, the calling still begs to be embraced.

Embracing the call and then moving into practical ministry deserves guidance so that those who are yet awaiting God's leader will not be damaged, disappointed or diluted in their communal calling.

Embracing the call and then moving into practical ministry deserves guidance so that those who are yet awaiting God's leader will not be damaged, disappointed or diluted in their communal calling. Exceptional clergy leaders surround themselves with wisdom. Even before Isaiah had a live coal touch his mouth, as a prophet Isaiah was surrounded by the wisdom of others who served God in like fashion.

"... Go and say to this people ..."

I suppose the question some are secretly pondering is whether or not God has slowed down on His recruitment process for Kingdom leadership. On the other hand, if by chance recruitment is still taking place is it possible to secure a viable placement for ministry purposes? The conversation between Isaiah and God concluded with Isaiah being commissioned and sent into his field of ministry. Isaiah did not leave his duties in the temple as one about to launch out on some kind of self-directed exploration. Isaiah's elevation into ministry beyond the original ministry assignment was on behalf of God, backed by God's power and voiced with God's words. For those who were the audience of Isaiah's ministry it would be clear that God had sent him into national leadership.

During this century, the church needs to be able to hear the voice of the Lord as God says for the leaders to "Go." The Kingdom of God in general and the Black church in particular is drastically facing a dearth of professional clergy leaders. In 1990, Lincoln and Mamiya made the following critique on the greatest need for the Black church. "If we were asked to make a single policy recommendation that we consider critical for the future of the Black church, it would be the need for more, better-trained, and better-educated Black clergy" (Lincoln and Mamiya 1992, p. 399). The spiritual economy of the Kingdom will collapse under outdated mechanics headed by period performance standards and expectations. God has a word for this people during this time that has been placed in the mouths of leaders who are yet to emerge.

With the proliferation of mega churches seeing congregations in excess of seven to twenty thousand attendees on a weekly basis, one might erroneously conclude that God no longer has need for a Kingdom recruitment process and that the needs of the Kingdom are now being served by a few well-endowed clergy persons. Should a spiritual feasibility study be conducted it would show proof that communities benefit from a collaboration of congregations representing small, large and the mega aggregations. In other words, even though there may be a church on every other block in your town, God is still saying "Go" to emerging Kingdom leaders.

The spiritual economy of the Kingdom will collapse under outdated mechanics headed by period performance standards and expectations.

The implementation of this apprenticeship model should deposit into the Kingdom

professional clergy leaders who are confident not only in their calling but also confident in their readiness. These leaders will be able to enter their responsibility better trained and most importantly, not alone. Along side of each will be another Isaiah who has the testimony of having heard the voice of the Lord, of having been groomed either directly or through divine exposure and of having been sent out by God.

CHAPTER 3

Biblical Foundations

*Unless the Lord builds the house, those who
build it labor in vain (Psalm 127:1).*

The foundational process for developing a clergy
apprenticeship model begins with an excavation
through biblical exegesis, historical reflection and
theological wisdom associated with leadership development.
Drawing from biblical examples of leadership development,
ideas will be erected which serve as structural support for the
reader's thinking about the importance of apprenticeship
and provide a variety of models to explore.

Clergy apprenticeship is not a new concept; however
its intentional implementation is an idea whose time has

come. The historical foundation provides a glimpse into the practice and results of informal leadership development that has been recently evidenced within the African Methodist Episcopal Church (AMEC). The reader should understand that similar training relationships take place within other denominations, and that the use of AMEC history does not in any way infer this phenomenon to be limited to any one denomination or one ethnicity.

Beyond thinking biblically and historically about the intentional practices of clergy apprenticeships, you are challenged to consider the theological necessity for this type of intentional development. Outlined here are current circumstances within the Kingdom of God that warrant a theological response to the place and privilege of investment, by established clergy, in the lives of new clergy leaders. Ideas will be presented that answer relevant questions of doctrinal issues connected with God and existing leader's participation in the training of new ministers.

Biblical Foundations

I began my research in this area by analyzing the biblical foundations for apprentice relationships, because I wanted to find out if mentoring is an optional activity or a ministerial responsibility directed by God in order to enlighten clergy leaders and give them biblical precedent to carry out this work. Psalm 119:105 says, "Your word is a lamp to my feet and a light to my path". For so many in the field of Kingdom leadership what I am presenting is in deed a brand new path. It is brand new not in concept but in application, in the intentionality of the application. Pastors know from first-hand experience how strong resistance can be when a new path is introduced. We rely on open hearts, pliable minds, ready spirits and sound biblical grounding in order to have the path traveled. I pray that once the light of God's word is shone upon this aspect of Kingdom leadership that experienced clergy leaders who prior to this point have not seen it as part of their divine mandate will begin to walk in the light by no longer dismissing participation as an optional activity.

For my research, Mentor-Apprentice models were selected based upon the leadership status of each person within the larger community of believers and an apparent as well as intentional bonding between each person. I investigated a comprehensive apprenticeship where each stage of development; call identification, mentoring and elevation are critical. Therefore biblical models that provided insight in each stage were selected. Other mentoring relationships can be observed in the canon, but were omitted here due to an absence of a previously determined qualifier. For example, Naomi and Ruth's relationship may be categorized as mentor-apprentice, however they were excluded here because their leadership was confined to the dynamics of the immediate family and not the community as a whole (Ruth 1:1-4:22).

Is mentoring an option or responsibility directed by God?

THE MOSES — JOSHUA MODEL

Concurrent Growth

Biblical examples from the Old and New Testament teach the attentive learner about leadership development

and apprenticeship training. The first and most subtle lesson is that effective mentoring is based in a wholesome relationship. Mentoring that takes place in the context of relationship allows for a dual result. In this atmosphere the mentor continues to develop concurrently as the apprentice is prepared for leadership. In the relationship between Moses and Joshua we see Joshua described as Moses' assistant (Exodus 24:13). Clearly, Moses is the mentor; however serving God as a deliverer was a new vocation for Moses and therefore an opportunity for his continued growth. Never before had Moses confronted the ruler of Egypt and demanded the release of his kinsmen (Exodus 6:11). Never before did Moses have an assistant on the order of Joshua. Although Aaron and Miriam assisted Moses with various aspects of leadership among the tribes, neither had the mantle of leadership which eventually manifested on Joshua's life. This also presented a growth experience for Moses as Joshua was being groomed for his destiny. Moses was relatively new at communicating vision, leading a congregation and instilling commitment to God's way of life. His calling to be a deliverer, nurturing the priestly call upon his brother,

> The first and most subtle lesson is that effective mentoring is based in a wholesome relationship.

while at the same time molding Joshua were all growth experiences for Moses; it was also a new experience for God's people. The people never had a leader like Moses. They had to formulate realistic expectations of Moses that were in line with God's assignment on his life. They also had to learn how to respect, interact with and follow their leader, and they had to relearn those same lessons once Joshua was elevated. The walk out of captivity and the journey to becoming a united community would require spiritual stretching from everyone starting with Moses through a succession of leaders.

Shared By Intention

The Moses-Joshua model of apprenticeship training demonstrates God's intention for leaders to share revelation, wisdom, responsibility and strategy. As God unfolds these components to the leader, God also intends for the apprentice to be included. When the Hebrew congregation confronted the turning points in their evolution, Joshua was recognized as an integral partner of the leadership team though still an apprentice.

> *Then Amalek came and fought with Israel at Rephidim. Moses said to Joshua, "Choose some men for us and go out, fight with Amalek. Tomorrow I will stand on the top of the hill with the staff of God in my hand." So Joshua did as Moses told him, and fought with Amalek, while Moses, Aaron, and Hur went up to the top of the hill. Whenever Moses held up his hand, Israel prevailed; and whenever he lowered his hand, Amalek prevailed. But Moses' hands grew weary; so they took a stone and put it under him, and he*

sat on it. Aaron and Hur held up his hands, one on one side, and the other on the other side; so his hands were steady until the sun set. And Joshua defeated Amalek and his people with the sword. Then the LORD said to Moses, "Write this as a reminder in a book and recite it in the hearing of Joshua: I will utterly blot out the remembrance of Amalek from under heaven (Exodus 17:8-14).

During the battle against the Amalekites, Moses trusts Joshua's judgment and therefore gives him the responsibility to select those men who would fight and ultimately win. After the victory, God insists that a record is maintained of their success and that the apprentice, Joshua, also hears the record. God intends for the apprentice to be included and not habitually excluded.

Moses possessed experiential knowledge about being in the presence of God. He knew that God's presence was a holy place and he also knew the appropriate response to the manifest glory of God's presence. At the high holy moment, when Moses ascended the mountain to receive the vision and mission for the congregation (the Ten Commandments), he took Joshua with him.

The Lord said to Moses, "Come up to me on the mountain, and wait there; and I will give you the tablets of stone, with the law and the commandment, which I have written for their instruction." So Moses set out with his assistant Joshua, and Moses went up into the mountain of God. To the elders he had said, "Wait here for us, until we come to you again; for Aaron and Hur are with you; whoever has a dispute may go to them" (Exodus 24:13).

The act of taking his apprentice with him into the presence of God demonstrated his intention to teach Joshua through personal example and exposure. In this one act, Moses models for Joshua exactly how he approaches God, waits on God, listens to God, responds to God, intercedes before God and departs from God's presence.

Spiritual growth between the mentor and apprentice is a continual and concurrent process. Moses openly shared his own spirituality with his apprentice but he also provided time and space for Joshua to develop and expand his connection with God. The Tent of Meeting was one such place where Joshua's spiritual sensitivity was facilitated and nurtured.

> Moses openly shared his own spirituality with his apprentice but he also provided time and space for Joshua to develop and expand his connection with God.

Now Moses used to take the tent and pitch it outside the camp, far off from the camp; he called it the tent of meeting. And everyone who sought the LORD would go out to the tent of meeting, which was outside the camp. Whenever Moses went out to the tent, all the people would rise and stand, each of them, at the entrance of their tents and watch Moses until he had gone into the tent. When Moses entered the tent, the pillar of cloud would descend and stand at the entrance of the tent, and the LORD would speak with Moses. When all the people saw the pillar of cloud standing at the entrance of the tent, all the people would rise and bow down, all of them, at the entrance of their tent. Thus the LORD used

*to speak to Moses face to face, as one speaks to a
friend. Then he would return to the camp; but his
young assistant, Joshua son of Nun, would not
leave the tent (Exodus 33:7-11).*

Some apprentices are called to lead within their
location of training and others are called to lead independent
of that location. Healthy mentoring relationships are
skilled at distinguishing the difference and are able to
recognize the appropriate time and season for transition.
Not all apprentices replace their mentors as leaders in the
congregations in which their training occurred but it did
happen in the case of Moses and Joshua. Elevating his
apprentice into the position of visionary leader took place
in a manner that was meaningful for both Joshua and the
congregation.

*The LORD said to Moses, "Go up this mountain
of the Abarim range, and see the land that I
have given to the Israelites. When you have seen
it, you also shall be gathered to your people, as
your brother Aaron was, because you rebelled
against my word in the wilderness of Zin when
the congregation quarreled with me. You did not
show my holiness before their eyes at the waters."
(These are the waters of Meribath-kadesh in
the wilderness of Zin.) Moses spoke to the LORD,
saying, "Let the LORD, the God of the spirits of all
flesh, appoint someone over the congregation who
shall go out before them and come in before them,
who shall lead them out and bring them in, so
that the congregation of the LORD may not be like
sheep without a shepherd." So the LORD said to
Moses, "Take Joshua son of Nun, a man in whom
is the spirit, and lay your hand upon him; have
him stand before Eleazar the priest and all the*

*congregation, and commission him in their sight.
You shall give him some of your authority, so that
all the congregation of the Israelites may obey. But
he shall stand before Eleazar the priest, who shall
inquire for him by the decision of the Urim before
the LORD; at his word they shall go out, and at
his word they shall come in, both he and all the
Israelites with him, the whole congregation." So
Moses did as the LORD commanded him. He took
Joshua and had him stand before Eleazar the priest
and the whole congregation; he laid his hands
on him and commissioned him—as the LORD had
directed through Moses (Numbers 27:12-23).*

People need leaders but they have a hard time
following leaders, especially when they are not confident
in the leader's origination or authority. The Hebrew
congregation was not present when God called and
commissioned Moses at the burning bush (Exodus 3:1-21)
but through the evidence of signs and wonders they came
to believe in the origination of Moses' leadership, even if
they did at times disrespect his authority. The Moses-Joshua
model demonstrates the impact of public elevation and
shared integrity upon a congregation and leader, especially
in the face of an enormous challenge.

*The LORD said to Moses, "Your time to die is near;
call Joshua and present yourselves in the tent of
meeting, so that I may commission him." So Moses
and Joshua went and presented themselves in the
tent of meeting, and the LORD appeared at the
tent in a pillar of cloud; the pillar of cloud stood at
the entrance to the tent. The LORD said to Moses,
"Soon you will lie down with your ancestors. Then
this people will begin to prostitute themselves to
the foreign gods in their midst, the gods of the*

land into which they are going; they will forsake me, breaking my covenant that I have made with them. My anger will be kindled against them in that day. I will forsake them and hide my face from them; they will become easy prey, and many terrible troubles will come upon them. In that day they will say, 'Have not these troubles come upon us because our God is not in our midst?' On that day I will surely hide my face on account of all the evil they have done by turning to other gods. Now therefore write this song, and teach it to the Israelites; put it in their mouths, in order that this song may be a witness for me against the Israelites. For when I have brought them into the land flowing with milk and honey, which I promised on oath to their ancestors, and they have eaten their fill and grown fat, they will turn to other gods and serve them, despising me and breaking my covenant. And when many terrible troubles come upon them, this song will confront them as a witness, because it will not be lost from the mouths of their descendants. For I know what they are inclined to do even now, before I have brought them into the land that I promised them on oath." That very day Moses wrote this song and taught it to the Israelites. Then the LORD commissioned Joshua son of Nun and said, "Be strong and bold, for you shall bring the Israelites into the land that I promised them; I will be with you" (Deuteronomy 31:14-23).

Joshua's elevation had to be a time of complex emotions. He is about to become what Moses had been for him and more; spiritual leader plus mighty warrior. As God elevates Joshua he provides Joshua with similar fore knowledge that Moses had at the beginning of his ministry.

*I know, however, that the king of Egypt will not
let you go unless compelled by a mighty hand. So
I will stretch out my hand and strike Egypt with
all my wonders that I will perform in it; after that
he will let you go (Exodus 3:19-20).*

God told Moses that Pharaoh would have a hard heart
but eventually they would be released from captivity.
Ministry assignments all have their periods of difficulty.
In this instance, God maximizes the moment of Joshua's
elevation by providing disclosure of the difficulties ahead
as well as the assurance that God would not leave Joshua
alone just like he never left Moses alone. The manner in
which God elevates Joshua also provides the people with
a witness that the trouble they will face is not a reflection
of the new leader, but in fact the consequence of their own
doing. Many a pastor can relate to instances when the
congregation seeks to place blame on the new leader for
their own sin and disobedience. God makes it clear during
Joshua's elevation that the trouble ahead is not because his
is not Moses. After Moses dies the people mourn and then
immediately respond to Joshua's leadership.

THE ELIJAH — ELISHA MODEL

Another Old Testament relationship that parallels
the apprenticeship process proposed in this study is seen
through the Elijah-Elisha model. I am not suggesting that
each step of identifying the call, mentoring and elevating
the apprentice is a ridged process. God is the originator of
the call to ministry and to Kingdom leadership; however
what I am proposing is that present leaders should, and can

become attentive observers to the work of the Holy Spirit. There is biblical precedent for expecting God to supply the Kingdom with apprentices who need to be identified,

The Elijah-Elisha model teaches the need for acute discernment and a willingness to reprioritize personal agendas in order for mentoring to accomplish God's goal

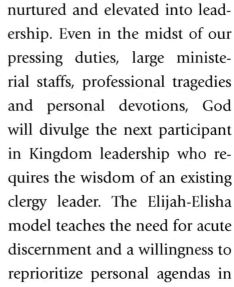

nurtured and elevated into leadership. Even in the midst of our pressing duties, large ministerial staffs, professional tragedies and personal devotions, God will divulge the next participant in Kingdom leadership who requires the wisdom of an existing clergy leader. The Elijah-Elisha model teaches the need for acute discernment and a willingness to reprioritize personal agendas in order for mentoring to accomplish God's goal.

More Than A Hobby

Preparing apprentices to be Kingdom leaders is not casual work and should not be viewed as an extracurricular activity in the vastness of daily ministry. Elijah was retreating from the landmark confrontation with the prophets of Baal (1 Kings 18: 20-40) when God identified the call to leadership on Elisha's life.

> *Also you shall anoint Jehu son of Nimshi as king over Israel; and you shall anoint Elisha son of Shaphat of Abel-meholah as prophet in your place. Whoever escapes from the sword of Hazael, Jehu shall kill; and whoever escapes from the*

*sword of Jehu, Elisha shall kill. Yet I will leave
seven thousand in Israel, all the knees that have
not bowed to Baal, and every mouth that has not
kissed him" (1 Kings 19: 16-17).*

Prior to God identifying Elisha as a future leader in
Israel's history, scripture does not give any indication that
an established relationship existed between Elijah and
Elisha, nor was Elisha readily available. The reasons why
God decided to use Elisha as a leader are not given. God
could have used other candidates that had demonstrated
their love and commitment to Elijah such as Obadiah but
God chose Elisha to be mentored by Elijah.

*Ahab summoned Obadiah, who was in charge
of the palace. (Now Obadiah revered the LORD
greatly; when Jezebel was killing off the prophets
of the LORD, Obadiah took a hundred prophets,
hid them fifty to a cave, and provided them with
bread and water)(1 Kings 18: 3-4).*

In the Elijah-Elisha model, the command was placed
upon Elijah, by God, to locate, anoint and apprentice
Elisha. Mentoring Elisha was not an option, it was Elijah's
responsibility.

*Then Elijah said to the people, "I, even I only,
am left a prophet of the LORD; but Baal's prophets
number four hundred fifty (1 Kings 18:22).*

*He answered, "I have been very zealous for the
LORD, the God of hosts; for the Israelites have
forsaken your covenant, thrown down your altars,
and killed your prophets with the sword. I alone*

*am left, and they are seeking my life, to take it
away" (1 Kings 19:10).*

In Elijah's mind, he was the only prophet who had
remained faithful to God (1 Kings 18: 22 and 1 Kings
19: 10). Driven by an inaccurate examination of God's
resources, Elijah could have concentrated all of his time,
skills and energy on the weightiness of his perceived
ministry responsibilities as the only remaining prophet.
Confronting government authorities, false religious
practices and rendering occasional pastoral sessions may
seem more urgent than the time-consuming involvement of
locating and establishing a relationship with an otherwise
unknown. Elijah's obedience recognizes the importance of
intentionally investing in the things that are intentional
with God.

Prepared for Replacement

*The company of prophets who were in Bethel came out
to Elisha, and said to him, "Do you know that today
the LORD will take your master away from you?" And
he said, "Yes, I know; keep silent" (2 Kings 2:3).*

The nature of their relationship as seen in 2 Kings
2 implies an apprenticeship that prepared Elisha to serve
in the Kingdom as a competent and exceptional prophet
to Israel. The community of leaders was knowledgeable
of the investment Elijah had placed in Elisha. They were
also discerning of the time and knew that it was the season
for transition. The respect and authority necessary to lead
was attributed to Elisha because people had witnessed his
connection with Elijah. We see evidence of the power of

association and the role it played in Elisha's elevation as a leader when Jehoshaphat seeks guidance from a prophet of the Lord.

> But Jehoshaphat said, "Is there no prophet of the Lord here, through whom we may inquire of the Lord?" Then one of the servants of the king of Israel answered, "Elisha son of Shaphat, who used to pour water on the hands of Elijah, is here." Jehoshaphat said, "The word of the Lord is with him."
>
> So the king of Israel and Jehoshaphat and the king of Edom went down to him (2 Kings 3:11-12).

Perhaps the most challenging aspect of the Elijah – Elisha model is the act of seeking out a person for whom a pre-existing relationship is not established, yet God has said clearly to you it is your responsibility to mentor them. Your immediate thought about mentoring may lean towards someone with an established connection to your ministry when in fact God could have someone else assigned to you for a particular season. Herein is another example of the non-negotiable quality of being able to hear the voice of the Lord.

THE JESUS — DISCIPLE MODEL

The calling of the first disciples distinguishes the Jesus-Disciple model as he identifies and selects his apprentices. In this model there is an element of clarity not previously seen between mentor and apprentice. The Jesus-Disciple model lays the foundation for the importance of clarity as it pertains to the goal and purpose of the mentoring relationship. Jesus tells Simon Peter that the result of their relationship is their transformation. The disciples do not fully grasp the magnitude of their transformation but they may conclude that their lives will be enhanced and that their presence in Jesus' life is not a frivolous existence.

Facilitated Learning

Once Jesus identified the disciples, they began a period of apprenticeship. For a season of time they sojourned with Jesus while he utilized every opportunity as a teaching moment. During this term of apprenticeship, Jesus facilitated an atmosphere for learning by allowing the disciples to comment and even criticize his actions. Not only did Jesus facilitate learning through observation, he also created an atmosphere that promoted self-exploration and discovery as seen in the following passage of scripture.

> *Immediately he made his disciples get into the boat and go on ahead to the other side, to Bethsaida, while he dismissed the crowd. After saying farewell to them, he went up on the mountain to pray. When evening came, the boat was out on the sea, and he was alone on the land. When he saw that they were straining at the oars against an adverse wind, he came towards them early in the morning, walking on the sea. He intended to pass them by. But when they saw him walking on the sea, they thought it was a ghost and cried out; for they all saw him and were terrified. But immediately he spoke to them and said, "Take heart, it is I; do not be afraid." Then he got into the boat with them and the wind ceased. And they were utterly astounded,*

*for they did not understand about the loaves, but
their hearts were hardened (Mark 6:45-52).*

Jesus' decision not to ride with them to Bethsaida
caused the disciples to discover their personal limitations
in a time of storm and they discovered the depths of their
hard heartedness. Both were lessons the disciples needed to
master before launching out into Kingdom leadership.

Following the identification of the disciples and a
season of intense spiritual and leader apprenticeship, Jesus
performs an inauguration of elevation whereby the new
leaders test what they have been learning.

*Then Jesus went about all the cities and villages,
teaching in their synagogues, and proclaiming
the good news of the kingdom, and curing every
disease and every sickness. When he saw the
crowds, he had compassion for them, because they
were harassed and helpless, like sheep without
a shepherd. Then he said to his disciples, "The
harvest is plentiful, but the laborers are few;
therefore ask the Lord of the harvest to send out
laborers into his harvest." Then Jesus summoned
his twelve disciples and gave them authority over
unclean spirits, to cast them out, and to cure
every disease and every sickness. These are the
names of the twelve apostles: first, Simon, also
known as Peter, and his brother Andrew; James
son of Zebedee, and his brother John; Philip and
Bartholomew; Thomas and Matthew the tax
collector; James son of Alphaeus and Thaddaeus:
Simon the Cananaean, and Judas Iscariot, the
one who betrayed him. These twelve Jesus sent
out with the following instructions: "Go nowhere
among the Gentiles, and enter no town of the*

Samaritans, but go rather to the lost sheep of the house of Israel. As you go, proclaim the good news, 'The kingdom of heaven has come near.' Cure the sick, raise the dead, cleanse the lepers, cast out demons. You received without payment; give without payment. Take no gold, or silver, or copper in your belts, no bag for your journey, or two tunics, or sandals, or a staff; for laborers deserve their food. Whatever town or village you enter, find out who in it is worthy, and stay there until you leave. As you enter the house, greet it. If the house is worthy, let your peace come upon it; but if it is not worthy, let your peace return to you. If anyone will not welcome you or listen to your words, shake off the dust from your feet as you leave that house or town. Truly I tell you, it will be more tolerable for the land of Sodom and Gomorrah on the day of judgment than for that town. "See, I am sending you out like sheep into the midst of wolves; so be wise as serpents and innocent as doves (Matthew 9:35-10:16).

As seen in Matthew 9:35-10:16 and Matthew 28:19-20, it is important to note that Jesus elevates the disciples while he is still alive to monitor their progress so that constructive guidance could still be applied to their development.

The challenge for current day professional clergy leaders desiring to mentor in light of the Jesus-Disciple Model is that of being relational and not yielding to the temptation of being creational. Jesus allowed the disciples to journey along with him, which created an avenue for him to be relational with his emerging leaders. Jesus' ability to be relational is also seen in his openness to hear their comments. In an atmosphere where questions are shunned or misunderstood as challenging authority, learning can be hampered. Although Jesus interpreted ministry experiences in light of spiritual truths, he did not attempt to re-create his apprentices in his own image of leader. In other words, Jesus allowed for their individuality to remain intact.

THE BARNABAS-PAUL-TIMOTHY MODEL

While they were worshiping the Lord and fasting, the Holy Spirit said, "Set apart for me Barnabas and Saul for the work to which I have called them (Acts 13:2).

Paul went on also to Derbe and to Lystra, where there was a disciple named Timothy, the son of a Jewish woman who was a believer; but his father was a Greek. He was well spoken of by the believers in Lystra and Iconium. Paul wanted Timothy to accompany him; and he took him and had him circumcised because of the Jews who were in those places, for they all knew that his father was a Greek (Acts 16: 1-3).

Barnabas and Paul's relationship, as well as Paul and Timothy's relationship are other examples of New Testament belief in the divine work to serve as a mentor and the benefits afforded to both the mentor and apprentice. Barnabas was an experienced and accepted leader among the followers of Christ when he initiated a mentoring relationship with Paul. The relationship, which would ultimately change in character, started after Paul's divine encounter with Jesus and the beginning of his preaching ministry.

Then Barnabas went to Tarsus to look for Saul, and when he had found him, he brought him to

Antioch. So it was that for an entire year they met with the church and taught a great many people, and it was in Antioch that the disciples were first called "Christians (Acts 11:25-26).

For an entire year Barnabas fed into Saul's spirit as his mentor while simultaneously developing a new congregation. According to Paul Moots, Barnabas was willing to take chances in order to expose Paul to the life of ministry, but he was also willing to accept God's direction for Paul as a separate journey (Moots 1999, p. 23). The separate journey that Paul would follow was not another process in being mentored but one of leadership. The time of transition was evident for both the mentor and apprentice. "Barnabas's relational insight was that Paul didn't need a mentoring, subordinate, or co-equal relationship; he needed to lead" (Clinton 1988, p. 104). Likewise when Timothy has been elevated to the responsibility of pastoral leadership Paul continues to mentor him with encouragement and wisdom (1 Timothy).

There are additional examples of mentoring models in scripture; however they do not emphasize mentoring for Kingdom leadership roles. During the time of captivity and release, God selected, trained and elevated Moses and Joshua to serve in the roles of leadership. During the time of religious synchronism on one extreme and apostasy at the other, God selected, trained and elevated Elijah and Elisha to serve in the roles of leadership. The ultimate work of establishing and growing a new belief system was accomplished using the roles of leadership that were selected, trained and elevated by Jesus and continued with the apostles.

Professional clergy leaders seeking to cast their mentoring style after the Barnabas – Paul – Timothy model will be challenged to accept their apprentice's shifting roles from student to peer and in some instances to mentor. Another challenging consideration is the exchangeable nature of leadership development. As the mentor you might begin the development process but along the way one of your former apprentices might take your student to a new or different direction. As long as the goal of Kingdom leadership remains the primary focus, the challenge of releasing an apprentice into the hands of another mentor or into the place of their assignment becomes an affirming step.

REVIEW

Based upon the biblical models of apprenticeship, there are indicators present that help to determine the nature of mentoring and lend insight on the place of primacy in the life of ministerial responsibility. Positive results can be achieved in an apprenticeship that is based in a wholesome relationship. In this environment of trust, the basic nature of mentoring thrives. Revelation, wisdom, responsibility and strategies are shared between mentors and apprentices. Both parties learn at the benefit of one another even when it means that personal agendas must be reprioritized. Apprenticeships are fluid in style therefore it is of paramount importance for mentors and apprentices to exercise discernment. Spiritual discernment is the aspect that allows for clarity, courage and confidence during the developmental process. Conclusions can be drawn concerning the monumental importance of developing new leaders, by the acts of Jesus, as he models the behavior of identifying the call, mentoring and elevating leaders for service within the Kingdom of God.

CHAPTER 4

Historical Foundations

I studied the historical foundation of clergy mentoring to demonstrate the impact that mentoring has upon the Kingdom of God, so that the present generation of leaders may learn from history and make the necessary adjustments to their present way of thinking in order that they may add exponentially to the pool of Kingdom leaders.

Historically, clergy leaders have benefited from informal apprentice relationships during their development even though written proof of these accounts is often nonexistent. To further complicate the matter of the absence of written accounts, during earlier decades, church leaders participated in similar activities but without the heading of mentor. It is difficult to chronicle an activity when the participants of the activity have not categorized their involvement. An example of this was seen when a clergy leader was asked to participate in the research of this project. There was a resounding opposition to the term of mentoring, declaring that the former pastor only provided an opportunity for exposure. Even when the title was removed and the activities of apprenticeship were described, the clergy leader remained in opposition to the idea that there had been an apprenticeship present in their leadership formation. I have not been able to adequately account for this type of resistance, but I do recognize that it may lend insight into a scarce body of written accounts of modern apprenticeships within the Kingdom of God.

The Bryant Legacy

The aim of my research was to develop a model that escaped the boundaries of denominational, cultural and ethnic walls without having to abandon the richness of an otherwise marginalized community. It is believed that a historical foundation based upon a Black church perspective is equally relevant to the larger body of writing within the Christian community. Using the recent history within the African Methodist Episcopal Church (AMEC), the Bryant Legacy is a prime documented example demonstrating the exponential effects of clergy apprenticeship and its impact upon the Kingdom of God (Mahlangu-Ngcobo 1992, pp. 26-29).

During the 2000 General Conference of the AMEC, Rev. Dr. Vashti McKenzie was elected as the church's first female bishop. Bishop McKenzie was not the first female to actively seek the elected office. In fact, during the 1996 General Conference there were two other women seeking the coveted position of being a bishop, and being the first female bishop in the AMEC. One of the candidates, Presiding Elder Carolyn Tyler, proved to be a qualified contestant with a strong voter selection after the first and second round of balloting. Candidate Tyler however did not gain the necessary votes to be elected a bishop in 1996 nor in 2000. However she was successful in 2004. What were the factors, aside from the providence of God, which benefited Rev. Dr. McKenzie and not Presiding Elder Tyler? One obvious factor was the visible support from a strong mentor-bishop presently seated on the bench of bishops.

> Bishops make bishops.

There is a common saying in the AMEC that "Bishops make bishops". The Bryant/Bryant/McKenzie connection is but only one example of this truism. Bishop John Bryant is himself the son of an AMEC bishop. Under his direct pastoral leadership and indirect clergy mentoring, several hundreds of preachers have accepted the call to ministry and Kingdom leadership. The placement success of Bishop Bryant's apprentices within Kingdom leadership has been noted across denominations. Bishop McKenzie is one of those who acknowledge him as her "father in the ministry". Bishop Bryant's exponential impact upon Kingdom leadership has even resulted in those who refer to him as their "grandfather in the ministry".

Spritual Parenting

The term, "father/mother in the ministry" is a commonly used descriptor when a preacher identifies who their pastor was when they received the call from God. Loosely used, the term attempts to draw a spiritual connection to an established ministry and most liberally, it seeks to infer an  apprenticeship between the pastor and new clergy person. However, drawing from the parallel of natural parental relationships, it takes more than the initial presence to really father/mother someone into maturity. To be a true father/mother in the ministry, as seen through the lenses of a mentoring model, requires an

> To be a true father/mother in the ministry requires an investment of time, a sharing of wisdom and intentional empowerment.

investment of time, a sharing of wisdom and intentional empowerment.

When Bishop McKenzie stood before the General Conference delegation and recited her acceptance speech, family members on one side and her mentor Bishop John R. Bryant, his wife Rev. Cecelia W. Bryant and their son Rev. Jamal H. Bryant flanked her on the other side. The fruit of a clergy apprenticeship was clearly visible. Bishop McKenzie acknowledged the spiritual presence of those who had paved the way for her but were now dead in Christ. It was evident to all witnesses that Bishop McKenzie was the beneficiary of an apprenticeship that resulted in her elevation to the office of bishop.

REVIEW

The phenomenon of clergy being elevated due to the edge that an apprenticeship provides is not restricted to the AMEC, but it is very common among the African American community. Eugene Gibson remarks that "deeply rooted into our mindset of being Africans in America are the concepts of the Master and the Apprentice and an unadulterated relationship with Deity" (Gibson 2002, p. 11). Over the years, terminology has changed but the premise is consistent. Those with knowledge take time to teach and prepare the young and spiritually eager. Transference of knowledge through apprenticeship has been such an expected part of the Christian culture until drawing attention to the activity appears to have been unnecessary. It is only through listening to the oral testimony of leaders that we are privileged to know about the forerunners in their lives. Historically, apprenticeships by any other name have existed whether in a formal sense or by way of informal casual relationships. Training in theological institutions has not always been available for some members of the religious community, but knowledge has been and will continue to be available as long as there remains an intentional act of sharing wisdom.

CHAPTER 5

Theological Foundations

I studied the theological framework of mentoring because I wanted to explore the doctrinal implications of identifying the call, mentoring and elevating women and men through a clergy apprenticeship and into transformational leadership, in order to determine if God's perspective on mentoring clergy leaders is that of an elective or required course of action to be executed by leaders in the Kingdom.

The Absence of Theological Discussion

A doctrinal statement on the role of leadership is not a subject that has gained vast attention from modern theologians.

What has been discovered is biblical exegesis under the heading of theological reflections. Patrick D. Miller, Jr., Princeton Theological Seminary Old Testament Theology professor, expressed an overall absence of theological reflection on the subject of clergy mentoring (Miller 2002). In his work on leadership theology, Miller also approaches the task as a biblical exegesis with an eye towards theology. Using four Old Testament examples of leadership, exercised by prophets, Miller begins a movement toward a theological understanding of leadership but stops short of a solid reflection (Miller 1992, p. 43). Modern scholars such as Aubrey Malphurs of Dallas Theological Seminary (Malphurs 2002), Randy McFarland of Denver Seminary (McFarland 2002) and Harold Westing, Sr., Denver Seminary Mentoring professor, (Westling 2002) all concur that skilled theological reflection in this area is desperately needed.

Speculations Concerning Theological Silence

I would speculate there are a few explanations for this omission. The first reason derives from a miscalculation of urgency. Canonical writings by New Testament leaders demonstrate that they exercised spiritual and organizational authority underneath an expectation that Jesus' return was looming. The ranks of leaders expanded in response to immediate growth from hearing the Christian message. But we are not given any indication that New Testament leaders expected Christ's return to take thousands of generations, thereby necessitating an intentional training process for replacement leaders. This was not a case of confused mortality in which the leaders lacked a realistic understanding of their participation in Kingdom advancement. Their history with

Jesus conditioned them to expect his second coming within the span of their leadership. His ministry with them was three years in length, his death took a few hours and his resurrection took three days. Under these standards, urgency for continuing to identify, train and elevate generations of new leaders did not exist.

The second hypothesis for a general omission may be based in the history of leadership positions that have been obtained and executed throughout dispensations, cultures and generations through lines of lineage. Leadership acquired through legacy guarantees passing the mantle of authority based upon family connection and not necessarily on God's calling and equipping. In this environment an urgency to identify, train and elevate generations of new leaders does not exist because the process automatically advances select individuals.

> Leadership acquired through legacy guarantees passing the mantle of authority based upon family connection and not necessarily on God's calling and equipping.

Another possible explanation for the lack of theological reflection on leadership mentoring may be the interpretation of Jesus' response to James, John and their mother.

> *Then the mother of the sons of Zebedee came to him with her sons, and kneeling before him, she asked a favor of him. And he said to her, "What do you want?" She said to him, "Declare that these two sons of mine will sit, one at your right hand and one at your left, in your kingdom." But Jesus answered, "You do not know what you are asking.*

Are you able to drink the cup that I am about to
drink?" They said to him, "We are able." He said
to them, "You will indeed drink my cup, but to sit
at my right hand and at my left, this is not mine
to grant, but it is for those for whom it has been
prepared by my Father." When the ten heard it,
they were angry with the two brothers. But Jesus
called them to him and said, "You know that the
rulers of the Gentiles lord it over them, and their
great ones are tyrants over them. It will not be so
among you; but whoever wishes to be great among
you must be your servant, and whoever wishes to
be first among you must be your slave; just as the
Son of Man came not to be served but to serve,
and to give his life a ransom for many (Matthew
20:20-28).

If Jesus is seen as speaking a scornful rebuke towards
ambitious requests to be leaders, then theologians may
not have considered reflection on this subject to be
noteworthy.

Theological Trailblazers

Pioneer is defined as one who ventures into
unexplored or unclaimed territory to settle (Webster 1984,
p. 894). A trailblazer therefore, is a pioneer in a specific field
of endeavor (Webster 1984, p. 1225). Without reservation,
the term theological trailblazer can be appropriately applied
to the first steps taken by Walton A. Williams and Don Payne
for their recent theological reflections on mentoring.

As a doctor of ministry candidate at Denver Seminary,
Walton Williams' makes the theological statement that,
"Due to the debilitating results of sin, training is vital for

effective ministry service and meaningful relationships. Jesus' recruitment of the Twelve clearly anticipated their need for ministry preparation. As the Master Teacher, His presence on earth marked the apex of equipping for ministry" (Williams 2001, p. 10). Although his dissertation does not fully develop this theological thought, a subsequent telephone discussion with Williams revealed agreement that further reflection is warranted (Williams 2002).

During the National Conference on Mentoring, sponsored by Denver Seminary, Don Payne, Suburban Training Center director, presented a lecture entitled, "A Theology of Mentoring". The following paraphrases represent excerpts from his lecture (Payne 2002). Payne presents a theological position that counters the "New Age" philosophy that seems pervasive in the board population of mentoring literature and recent Christian literature. Payne believes that current writings on mentoring, broad and Christian are strongly influenced by the "New Age" quest of self-discovery through introspection leading to self-actualization. In this paradigm, mentoring provides the tools and techniques to get in touch with oneself. Fulfillment then becomes a validation of personal values but not a challenge, and empowerment is the act of helping to realize personal values. Payne argues against the assumption that the "self" can be fulfilled in isolation and by one's own resources.

Against this "contra-communal" philosophy of mentoring, Payne raises a Trinitarian approach. Viewing the Trinity as persons in communion, Payne states that humanity, in the image of God, is interdependent. Personal formation then means that we cannot actualize ourselves apart from the community of faith. In the Trinitarian paradigm, fulfillment is evidenced by growth in our motivation to love and empowerment occurs when the mentor recognizes God's power active in the life of the apprentice.

Payne also applies the doctrine of the incarnation to address issues of power that are inherent to mentoring. Whereas pop-cultural mentoring may be used to accumulate layers of insight, control and leverage, personified mentoring emerges from suffering and struggle. Payne suggests that in mentoring, personified power is the ability to know and follow the will of God.

The groundbreaking work begun by Williams and Payne is inspiring for those who are distinctly interested in a theological perspective on mentoring. James Evans has stated that, "Theology is essentially the church's response to the autobiographical impulse, and it grows out of the need to proclaim with authority and commitment the identity and mission of the church in the world. That is, in theology, the church both asks and answers the questions, 'Who are we, and where are we going?'" (Evans 1992, p. 1). Perhaps it is a rare occasion that a person recognizes the oddity of their calling at the onset, and is accepting of the title "trailblazer". It is with a courageous spirit, and I pray, an intellectual anointing, that I mount the platform as a trailblazer in the area of theological reflections on clergy leadership mentoring. The following theological foundations presented here add to the work begun by Williams and Payne, in an effort to answer Evans' questions of "Who are we (as clergy leaders) and where are we (clergy leaders) going in our development?"

Toward A Theology of Mentoring

Establishing a theological foundation for leadership mentoring will begin with the identity of leadership, both person and function. What is leadership in the biblical witness and are there any patterns that could suggest how these leaders should be identified, trained and elevated? This next component of theological reflection seeks to discover the existing conditions in the Kingdom of God today that necessitate an intentional apprenticeship program for clergy leaders. Although modern theologians have not readily communicated a theology of clergy leader apprenticeship, there are associated doctrines that inform our interpretation of events and process, which surface during a leader's development journey.

The Providence Of God

The providence of God is one such doctrine that is woven throughout the identification, training and elevation of leaders in the Kingdom of God. God's providence has been described as follows: "God is continually involved with all created things in such a way that He (1) keeps them existing and maintaining the properties with which He created them; (2) cooperates with created things in every action, directing their distinctive properties to cause them to act as they do; and (3) directs them to fulfill His purposes" (Grudem 1994, p. 315). If we believe, even when it is not evident to us, that God is working all events according to God's own will, then we must also believe that the details of identifying, training and elevating clergy leaders are all birthed in the heart of

God. Our perspective may not clearly observe God's direct involvement or God's ultimate intentions as it concerns the various events experienced in leadership development. Our inability to perceive God's orchestration does not negate God's involvement.

The biblical witness of how nations, congregations and existing leaders identify the call of God upon an apprentice varies depending on God's perceived direct or indirect involvement. In the Old Testament, God initiates both direct contacts with the new leader via dream, epiphany or vision, then communicates the assignment and God makes indirect contact through the use of an existing leader. In the latter case, existing leaders serve as a messenger to announce the identity of the apprentice and anoint them for service. The congregations, who must also identify or acknowledge the aspiring leader, were not always present when God directly commissioned the leader, as in the case of Moses (Exodus 3:1-18), but once the leader presented themselves the people accepted their position and submitted to their leadership. This acceptance was due in part because Old Testament congregations lived with an expectation that God would provide anointed leadership. Therefore, since the people were predisposed to anticipating a leader, a spirit of suspicion did not control their response to those who publicly acknowledged God's call upon their life. They embraced new leadership as a part of God's providence.

Old Testament patterns of training new leaders are influenced by the providence of God and the work of the Holy Spirit. One such phase of the pattern occurs when God and the new leader are journeying through development independent of the participation of others. In this instance it is the work of the Holy Spirit, communicating directly with the new leader that instructs, corrects and shares the vision of God for the people as was the case with Ezekiel.

> *He said to me: O mortal, stand up on your feet, and I will speak with you. And when he spoke to me, a spirit entered into me and set me on my feet; and I heard him speaking to me. He said to me, Mortal, I am sending you to the people of Israel, to a nation of rebels who have rebelled against me; they and their ancestors have transgressed against me to this very day. The descendants are impudent and stubborn. I am sending you to them, and you shall say to them, "Thus says the Lord GOD." Whether they hear or refuse to hear (for they are a rebellious house), they shall know that there has been a prophet among them. And you, O mortal, do not be afraid of them, and do not be afraid of their words, though briers and thorns surround you and you live among scorpions; do not be afraid of their words, and do not be dismayed at their looks, for they are a rebellious house. You shall speak my words to them, whether they hear or refuse to hear; for they are a rebellious house. But you, mortal, hear what I say to you; do not be rebellious like that rebellious house; open your mouth and eat what I give you. I looked, and a hand was stretched out to me, and a written scroll*
>
> *was in it. He spread it before me; it had writing on the front and on the back, and written on it were words of lamentation and mourning and woe. Ezekiel 2:1-10*

The particular lessons of leadership development are designed in accordance with the immediate situation, the personality of the leader and other unknown factors that are only understood by God. In the case where God includes an existing leader as a part of the development process, we see that by way of the Holy Spirit working in and through people and events, the apprentice learns from observation, co-participation and then replication.

The Sovereignty Of God

The doctrines of omnipotence and sovereignty are closely related. Omnipotence means that "God is able to do all God's holy will and sovereignty has been defined as God's exercise of power (God's rule) over God's creation" (Grudem 1994, p. 216). If we believe that God is able to exercise power in order to accomplish God's holy will, then we must also accept God's methodology, no matter how strange or undesirable it may present itself.

Old and New Testament patterns of elevating new leaders usually required the life event of death. Joshua was elevated after the death of Moses. Samuel was elevated after the death of Eli and the disciples were fully elevated after the death of Jesus. The event of death was predominately physical but in some instances the physical death was preceded by spiritual dullness or spiritual death. In either case, the new leader was elevated when God determined that the season was appropriate. It is difficult to say with absolute certainty which preconditions determined a shift in leadership. In the example of Moses, which reality determined the timing for God to be revealed at the burning bush? Had the intensity of the Hebrews' cry for deliverance become unbearable to the point of needing Moses to be elevated as a leader, or was the timing determined by Moses' state of readiness? The only pattern evident in the timing for elevating new leaders rests in the sovereignty of God. God determined when a transition from old to new leadership would take place; however, once that determination was made the shift was meaningful for both the leader and nation or congregation.

The New Testament patterns of identifying, training and elevating new leaders is analogous to the Old Testament in many ways. Jesus identifies disciples and communicates the assignment, which for the first three years consists of journeying with Jesus and at the appropriate time he elevates them, prior to the crucifixion and with the great commission, to perform their responsibility. In Jesus' absence the providence of God is clearly evident when the leaders are faced with the decision of replacing Judas. Casting lots was an act of faith that God, through providence, would reveal the identity of the new leader.

New Testament patterns for training leaders embraced a method of apprenticeship. The disciples learned by the example of Jesus as seen through the daily routine of his life and ministry. Throughout the entire span of Jesus' ministry, the disciples were witnesses to the work of the Holy Spirit in the ministry of the great commission (Mark 16:14-18). In the case of the apostle Paul we also see the Holy Spirit as the informing force who provides training for ministry. After submitting to God, Paul departs for a period of three years, and receives revelations from the Holy Spirit. The time spent under the guidance of the Holy Spirit provided Paul with the essential foundation for his ministry assignment.

New Testament patterns of elevating new leaders continued to rely upon the providence of God. There is the pattern of God revealing to the leaders that the season for

elevation is present and then there is also the pattern of recognized elevation. The pattern of recognized

The pattern of recognized elevation describes the dynamic when people begin to comprehend and accept the elevation that God has already set in motion.

elevation describes the dynamic when people begin to comprehend and accept the elevation that God has already set in motion. After Jesus' death and accession, the community began to perceive the disciples as apostles. In the minds of the people, the disciples had transitioned from

being followers of Jesus to being leaders of his gospel. The same can be said for Paul in connection with his relationship with the apostles. Although God elevated Paul to be an apostle, recognized elevation occurred when Barnabas took Paul and presented him before the counsel in Jerusalem.

> *When he had come to Jerusalem, he attempted to join the disciples; and they were all afraid of him, for they did not believe that he was a disciple. But Barnabas took him, brought him to the apostles, and described for them how on the road he had seen the Lord, who had spoken to him, and how in Damascus he had spoken boldly in the name of Jesus. So he went in and out among them in Jerusalem, speaking boldly in the name of the Lord (Acts 9:26-28).*

Existing Ethos in Kingdom Leadership

The need for current Kingdom leaders to become

intentional in their mentoring practices is fueled by the cry from the next generation. Women and men who are young in the ministry are looking around the landscape and are frustrated with the absence, and in some cases, indifference, of the elders. When fathers and mothers in the faith cease to parent the offspring of new leaders, it doesn't mean that new leaders will uniformly streak from their calling, it just means they may not come forward with the degree of preparation otherwise attainable. Fortunately, the church is a forgiving and patient organism, which makes room for trial and error. However forgiving the church may be, the stewardship of our time is inadequately used when an apprenticeship could have provided an opportunity to avoid the inevitable mistakes that a lack of wisdom produces.

Shortfalls of Theological Education

Intentional training of Kingdom leaders is necessitated by the dilemmas presented in light of organized religion and the shortfalls of theological education. Organizing religion into denominations has helped to propel the various belief systems within each denomination, but at the same time it has handicapped the next generation in terms of knowing how to navigate through the structure. Interpreting the call and work of God through the lenses of denominational creeds and disciplines is far less fluid than the Old and New Testament patterns of following the leading of the Holy Spirit. Apprenticeships serve as a conduit for transmitting knowledge that is necessary for success within organized structures. Additionally, apprenticeships are necessary because they supplement the academic training provided by theological institutions, an education that is deemed insufficient in the minds of some.

Cornel West is one such theologian who is critical of the quality and usefulness of the training provided by theological institutions. West spreads the crisis among three areas: the double consciousness of the academy, a lack of autonomous subject matter and a student body that is the product of our advanced capitalist culture. West is convinced that an apprenticeship is valuable for helping students deal with the burden of molding their ministry in the current age (West 1988, p. 276).

Relationship as the Ideal

> 'You shall love the Lord your God with all your heart, and with all your soul, and with all your mind.' This is the greatest and first commandment. And a second is like it: 'You shall love your neighbor as yourself.' On these two commandments hang all the law and the prophets (Matthew 22:36-40).

Biblical patterns for identifying, training and elevating new leaders suggests models for how the present generation of Kingdom leaders may be intentional in this same area of responsibility, especially in light of the current state of Kingdom leadership. Within the Kingdom of God there resides an assumption that our lives are interconnected and that the basis for our activities is relationship. Relationship between humanity and God exists due to the atonement provided by Jesus (John 1:14). As Christians, our relationships with one another exists due to the love and command from Jesus. Our expressed understanding of relationship influences how we support one another during times of weakness, sickness, joy, victory and searching, and molds an evolving Christian personality. Unfortunately the current culture, enforced with thoughts of individualism, belief systems that shadow humanism and overall social disorganization, has infected the state of relationship, even in the Kingdom of God. The texture of ministry has become commercial and competitive. It appears that a present approach to pastoral theology is influenced more by individual achievement and thus reduces clergy leadership development to a ritual marked by the receipt of ordination documents (Schnase 1993).

Relationally Broken

Relational leadership has been altered by the thirst for personal accolades and compounded by the damaging residuals of suspicion and mistrust. To our account, it is easy to conclude that Christians in general, and clergy in particular, have more confidence in the power of the sin within the hearts of fellow Christians than in the power of the Holy Spirit. Confidence in the power of sin is an offspring of previous experiences of sabotage, deception and disappointment. When a leader's trust has suffered the violence of manipulation and malice, their protection mechanism serves to erect walls of insulation. Circumstances such as these make it difficult for leaders to invest themselves in the lives of new leaders. Not only are current leaders faced with the challenge of investing themselves in the lives of new leaders, they must first embody concern for the state of someone's ministry other than their own.

In order to do this, leaders must be able to look beyond the primordial system of survival of the fittest and see a more excellent way of fitness of the Kingdom.

Reversed Pendulum

Kingdom fitness is attained when there is an interconnection between generations whereby wisdom is capable of flowing from the elders. A biblical picture of this transference of wisdom is seen throughout the book of Proverbs. Wisdom is portrayed as a woman, and the children are encouraged to heed the father's (elders) teachings as it pertains to the benefits, value and insights that wisdom provides.

> *Listen, children, to a father's instruction, and be attentive, that you may gain insight; for I give you good precepts: do not forsake my teaching. When I was a son with my father, tender, and my mother's favorite, he taught me, and said to me, "Let your heart hold fast my words; keep my commandments, and live" (Proverbs 4:1-40).*

The overall understanding from this passage, and many others like it, is that the father, or elder person, desires to pass onto the child (next generation) the accumulation of what has been learned throughout a lifetime. The passing of wisdom is practiced from generation, to generation, to generation. It was important for the child to possess this wisdom because it would one day become their responsibility to care for the family unit. As an act of extended provision, the elder recognizing their responsibility was able to ensure the well being of the family by preparing the next leader. What we do not see in the biblical context, but is ever present in our current context, is the image of the children having to compel or beg the elders to pass down wisdom. The assumption is that the elder is eager to teach and the children are exhorted to listen and remember. But in our current context of clergy leadership, the pendulum has swung in the opposite direction leaving the children in ministry exhorting the elders to speak the wisdom and provide insight. Felisha Carson sounds a similar cry for clergy elders when she wrote:

> As a single African American seminarian, I have longed for mentors who have been here and done this, who have wisdom that can be passed on to those of us who are working our way through this journey. It would be a blessing to have someone who can help make sense out of these peculiar (ministry) experiences. With the gifts granted us for the edification of the entire Kingdom of God, we as a people can bless so many others. Seminarians need all of you who are mature on the journey to encourage, pray for, and console them (Carson 2002, p. 11).

Stewardship — A Theological Framework for Clergy Mentoring

God gave ministry gifts to the church, "the gifts he gave were that some would be apostles, some prophets, some evangelists, some pastors and some teachers" (Ephesians 4:11). Those gifts were given to fulfill God's holy will "to equip the saints for the work of ministry, for building up the body of Christ" (Ephesians 4:12). These ministry gifts themselves need to be built up to a place of maturity in order for them to aptly assume their divine purpose of Kingdom leadership. Until such time, they are entrusted into the hands of their clergy leaders otherwise known as the apostle, prophet, evangelist, pastor and/or teacher in their lives.

From God's perspective, the clergy leader has been given a precious and valuable gift, in the form of a person, to be stewarded. Identifying the call, mentoring and elevating women and men into transformational leadership is an act of good stewardship. To not participate in this fashion, but instead to ignore the call, dismiss the need for mentoring or abdicate the responsibility in elevating women and men into leadership, is equivalent to digging a hole in the ground and hiding the Lord's gifts (Matthew 25:14-18). Clergy leaders are influential, they help chart the course in the lives of God's people. Clergy leadership is a privilege; they serve at God's pleasure. Clergy leadership is rewarding and at the same time, very costly.

> That slave who knew what his master wanted, but did not prepare himself or do what was wanted will receive a severe beating. But the one who did not know and did what deserved a beating will receive a light beating. From everyone to whom much has been given, much will be required; and from the one to whom much as been entrusted, even more will be demanded (Luke 12:47-48).

From a moral perspective, clergy leaders must submit to their obligation:

Those of us who have inherited opportunities

and sponsorship that we never deserved or earned are morally bound to enable those who inherited disadvantages and obstacles that they did not deserve or earn to achieve the same outcomes that we are enabled to achieve, with our unearned and undeserved opportunities and sponsorship
(Proctor 1989, p. 150).

Renewal — A By-product of Mentoring

Clergy leaders are not capable of avoiding their role in the developmental process of women and men entering ministry. No matter how preoccupied a person may be with actualizing his or her own vision in ministry, the impact is inescapable. "When God calls you to be a leader, whether you like it or not, you will become a mentor to those who listen to you, are affiliated with you and who watch you (Jacobs 1995, p. 115). Living a life of clergy leadership is tantamount to enabling God's purpose. God is continually involved in the formation of our lives

Living a life of clergy leadership is tantamount to enabling God's purpose.

and the health of the Kingdom. The appearance of God's involvement is incalculable. The only certainty is that God's providential involvement and sovereign power are directing leaders to prepare the church for Jesus' return. The leader's journey is not a road of ease and endless luxury. And while God is bountifully empowered, a person is subject to become scared, discouraged, disillusioned and depressed.

Identifying the call, mentoring and elevating women and men into transformational leadership is an opportunity for the leaders to become personally, spiritually and emotionally regenerated. Speaking to a gathering of approximately 3,000 women at a spiritual retreat, Dr. Claudette Copeland used the relationship between Naomi and Ruth to demonstrate the dynamic of renewal when the elders mentor the younger persons that God places under their influence. Dr. Copeland states, "God put the hunger (for mentoring) in Ruth to rekindle the purpose in Naomi, because Naomi was too bitter, tired and angry to reach out to Ruth" (Copeland 1998). The circumstances of Naomi's life left her scared and unenthusiastic about her future. Naomi was certainly too encumbered with her own life to give attention to Ruth's future. In joining and continuing the bond between the two women, Dr. Copeland lifts the concept that "God is attaching the past to the future, wisdom to strength" (Copeland 1998). Through the process of affecting Ruth's life, Naomi is restored to a better place.

> So Boaz took Ruth and she became his wife. When they came together, the Lord made her conceive, and she bore a son. Then the women said to Naomi, "Blessed be the Lord, who has not left you this day without next-of-kin; and may his name be renowned in Israel! He shall be to you a restorer of life and a nourisher of your old age; for your daughter-in-law who loves you, who is more to you than seven sons, has borne him". Then Naomi took the child and laid him in her bosom, and became his nurse. The women of the neighborhood gave him a name, saying, "A son has been born to Naomi" (Ruth 4:13-17).

I believe that leadership is a gift to the church, given by God, for the work of ministry and edifying of its citizens

(Ephesians 4:11-12). I further believe that leaders are persons called by God to accomplish the responsibility of equipping the congregation in their interaction with God.

The charismatic community has written on the topic of Kingdom leadership from a biblical basis and has identified Kingdom leaders as those whom God has called to be apostles, prophets, pastors, evangelists or teachers. The office in which they occupy determines the function of their leadership. For example, according to David Cannistraci, "Apostles serve together with the prophet to lay the foundation for the entire temple of God, while receiving alignment and positioning from Jesus" (Cannistraci 1996, p. 82). In quoting Peter Wagner, Cannistraci further defines apostles as:

> The gift of apostle is the special ability that God gives to certain members of the Body of Christ to assume and exercise general leadership over a number of churches with an extraordinary authority in spiritual matters that is spontaneously recognized and appreciated by those churches. Apostles are those whom God has given especially to pastors and church leaders. They are those to whom pastors can go for counsel and help. They are peacemakers, troubleshooters and problem solvers. They can make demands that may sound autocratic but that are gladly accepted because people recognize the gift and the authority it carries with it. They have the overall picture in focus and are not restricted in vision to the problems of the local church (Cannistraci 1996, pp. 91-92).

Other contemporary writers, including sociologists,

classify leadership by individual aptitudes. Writers such as John Maxwell and George Barna use this approach to equip the church with qualified leadership. While both groups of interpreters have convincing descriptions, the reader is abandoned to decipher if the groups are identifying the same segment of the church population. There does not appear to be a panel discussion between groups, on leaders and leadership in the Kingdom of God.

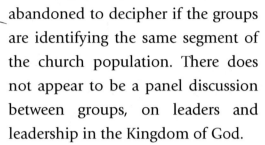

Investing in the leadership potential of new clergy leaders is a matter of professional and Kingdom stewardship.

God has demonstrated a pattern of providing human leadership, those who represent and work along with God to accomplish the purposes of the Kingdom. In so doing, we as Christian believers are able to rely and anticipate that new leaders will need formal education and informal development in order to navigate the terrain of ministry. Providing healthy training through a relational model can be difficult because of the conditioning of our current culture, perceived self-importance and professional wounds from the past. For those who gather the personal conviction and courage to invest in the development of another leader, the results are exponential for producing quality and quantity leaders in the Kingdom of God. Investing in the leadership potential of new clergy leaders is a matter of professional and Kingdom stewardship.

Although greater theological attention is needed, the revelation available to us through biblical, historical and theological foundations set the stage for understanding the nature of leadership.

CHAPTER 6

Other Voices Speak

In the first chapter, the rationale was introduced for developing an intentional and methodical model to be used by clergy in their work of identifying, mentoring and elevating women and men into transformational leadership. Evidence from outside of the church, such as rating polls conducted by Ebony magazine (Kinnon 1997, p. 102) communicate the perception that some ministers are more capable and effectual than others in their work of Kingdom leadership. What are the components that separate the successful from the incidental? Whereas some Kingdom leaders have experienced public recognition for their service in ministry, still others who have a call to serve God never reach the potential of that particular calling. Aspiring and established clergy need the wisdom of Kingdom elders. Providing an apprenticeship for women and men called to Kingdom leadership is a step beyond the ordination process and formalized theological education. It is a step towards healthy ministry facilitated by whole leaders.

The historical and biblical witness presented in previous chapters supports the conviction that God provides believers with human leadership. Those who serve in the role of leadership do so with the calling and equipping that is commensurate for partnership with God. Proficiency in leadership is the result of traversing a continual learning curve that consumes bountiful amounts of time, intention and spiritual resources.

The concept of mentoring is a key component of the model developed from this research; however, the term is stretched to encompass the intentional identification and elevation of women and men into Kingdom leadership. This level of deliberate involvement in the development of God's chosen leaders has both biblical and historical precedents but minuscule theological reflections associated with it. Clearly, this is an area that cries out for attention from the theological community.

Researching the intentional practices of professional clergy who identify, mentor and elevate women and men through a clergy apprenticeship and into transformational leadership has resulted in a model, which is believed to be an effective process for accomplishing the stated goal. This model uses a teaching method that has been proven to be appropriate for adult learners. It is relationally based in design and application and it is also very challenging for both mentors and apprentices.

Leadership is a gift to the church, given by God and the time has long passed for attention to be placed upon preparing new leaders in a way that is holistic. This researcher is not the first to hear God's holy whisper as it pertains to clergy development through the process of apprenticeship or mentoring. In recent years there has been increased attention in this area, though the focus has been slightly different than the focus of this research. In this chapter, some of the recent examinations will be reviewed and in many cases, built upon, to position a stable foundation for the mentoring model developed from this research.

In this chapter the process of development is examined from the perspective of popular notions in the secular environment and the sacred tradition. In particular, concepts such as mentoring, coaching and transformational leadership are examined. The foundations presented will explain how God's method of developing leaders, if yielded to, will provide the Kingdom with the type of visionaries necessary for the work at hand.

THE PROCESS OF DEVELOPMENT

Mentoring: Secular versus Sacred

The leadership development activity, sometimes known as mentoring, has begun to attract the attention of those who study and treasure sacred matters. In their research, literature from the educational, corporate and government arenas seem to dominate the discussion concerning the justification for mentoring, as well as the methods and results of mentoring. "Originating from ancient Greek mythology, mentoring has experienced a pinnacle of expansion and research attention during the last decade. Not only business and education, but various departments of the United States government are now prominent advocates of mentoring. It is estimated that one third of America's major firms have mentoring programs in which executives guide and counsel younger employees who show promise" (Williams 2001, p. 90).

In doctoral research that coupled mentoring with persuasive messages to increase relational evangelism, Jeffery Gill has observed, "As society continues to change over the generations, new methods are discovered and old methods are rediscovered. Psychologists and sociologists have discovered that during the early seasons of life, especially childhood through early middle age, young men and women need mentors. Realizing Western culture has promoted academic, lecture-oriented forms of educating, a void for training via relationships has resulted" (Gill 1997, p. 53).

John Sweetman was also able to make this determination while conducting research for his doctor of ministry studies. He created a self-study course designed to develop mentoring competencies for the church environment. Sweetman (1999), building on the work of Murray and Owen (1991), Healy and Welchart (1990), and Nash and Treffinger (1991), observed an increased interest in facilitated mentoring relationships. Beginning in the corporate arena, the interest quickly gained momentum in government, schools, colleges and universities. Pragmatic considerations proved to be the motivating force when businesses began to pursue mentoring.

According to Sweetman's research, secular organizations have many different concepts of what is expected to occur under the heading of mentoring. Citing the work of Cohen and Galbraith, Sweetman integrates their definitions of mentoring with his own. According to Cohen and Galbraith, after reviewing definitions from the literature in nine different fields, common "themes" run through the definitions. These themes include:

1. Mentoring is a process within a contextual setting.
2. Mentoring involves a relationship of a more knowledgeable individual with a less experienced individual.
3. Mentoring provides professional networking, counseling, guiding, instructing, modeling and sponsoring.
4. Mentoring is a developmental mechanism (personal, professional and psychological).
5. Mentoring is a socialization and reciprocal relationship.
6. Mentoring provides an identity transformation for both mentor and mentee.

Sweetman believed that the only concept raised by Cohen and Galbraith that is not apparent in the definition of mentoring used in his project is the benefit of the relationship to the mentor as well as the mentoree. "Perhaps the definition would have been enhanced by the defining of mentoring as a "mutual", relational experience. Therefore Christian mentors are committing themselves to a mutual, relational experience through which the mentor empowers the mentoree by sharing God-given resources" (Sweetman

1999, pp. 97-98).

Although the definitions of mentoring might identify common activity, the question raised in this research is whether or not the end results hold all things in common. Don Payne approaches this concern from a different angle when he argues that Christian mentoring must be distinct in its activity otherwise we have only succeeded in baptizing a secular practice with Christian terminology (Payne 2002). The distinctiveness that is needed is available when Christ remains the cornerstone of the mentoring activity.

Secular enterprises shape their executives in a fashion that exalts traits, standards and goals that are often antithetical to the Kingdom of God. One particular area where secular and sacred leadership development differs is in personal development. Gill remarks that, "Without question, personal development should accompany career development. Sadly, some in the pursuit of success in their careers hinder personal development in areas related to family, growth in other relationships and spiritual growth. They have divorced "what they do" from "who they are." In doing so, whether one is a mentor or protégé, he has missed the greatest benefit of mentoring"(Gill 1997, p. 59).

Coaching — The First Cousin of Secular Mentoring

In an issue of *Current Thoughts & Trends* magazine, the topic of mentoring and other disciplines associated with it were discussed at length. Coaching was one of the alternative occupations that was reviewed. Coaching is an activity that provides mentoring type interaction at a negotiated market price. According to the article, coaching has soared in significance. "Around the country, many therapists are abandoning their practices in favor of a creative variation: coaching. Both disciplines are intertwined, but coaching differs from psychotherapy in that coaching has less to do with pathology and more to do with nurturing untapped human strength. It is about mindset rather than method. The movement has become so popular that some say coaching may well become the most significant human services profession of the 21st century" (Dean 2002, p. 14).

Corporate Mentoring Solutions, Inc. draws a connection between mentoring and coaching: "As a subset activity of mentoring, coaching is organized to enhance the understanding and use of an innovation, skill or even a specific strategy. Coaching is a cyclical process designed to extend ordinary training (which is often done in the mass, classroom setting)" (Corporate Mentoring Solutions 2002, p. 5).

Organizations abound on the Internet promoting the profession of coaching or life strategist. The Spencer Institute is another example of the growing trend. Their homepage provides the following description of coaching, "In the past, many people did some form of coaching, but did not call themselves coaches. The field as we know it started in the early 1980s. Prior to the term 'coaching,' people referred to themselves as mentors, consultants, advisors or just a helping hand. Today, coaching is a more highly recognized and respected occupation. Since coaching is not sports psychology or psychotherapy, there are no state or regional laws for 'coaching' someone on important issues in their life. As a whole, coaches are allies to those who seek their advice and guidance. A coach will assess and align their client's goals, beliefs, values, morals and support system.

The coach will create a plan of action while guiding and motivating the client to reach set goals" (Spencer Institute 2002, p. 1).

The secular climate is thirsty for results oriented paths that lead to professional success, individual achievement and all of the trappings that are associated with this image. To this end, persons who intertwine mentoring with coaching market spiritual quests, absent the divine presence and significance of Jesus Christ. In this atmosphere it is clear why Payne warns Christians about the hazards of co-mingling secular mentoring with sacred mentoring.

Coaching is an avenue of spiritual formation when Christ is present in the developmental process.

> When the bases of operational and spiritual development are Christological, then coaching becomes aligned with true sacred mentoring.

One should not assume that all forms of spiritual formation are Christian based. Neither can the assumption be asserted concerning coaching. However, when the bases of operational and spiritual development are Christological, then coaching becomes aligned with true sacred mentoring.

Sacred Shaping

The cultural climate plays a significant impact upon how persons are shaped for leadership and the type of leadership they will engage. Reggie McNeal makes this point when analyzing Apostle Paul's entrance into Christianity, "Paul's meteoric rise in pharisaic Judaism did not set the pace for his leadership ascendance in Christianity. In each case, God had work to do — sometime in the leader's world, always in the leader's heart" (McNeal 2000, p. 57).

For the Kingdom leader, preparation is beyond the matters of academic astuteness although study is certainly a requirement (2 Tim. 2:15). An intellectual caution needs to be sounded because it is easy for a person to matriculate through biblical scholarship and not be touched internally by the essence of the word of God. However, for those who are representatives of God and God's purposes, the foundation of their preparation is a matter of shaping ones' heart. The heart is devious above all else; it is perverse, who can understand it? (Jeremiah 17:9). Without the shaping, or reshaping of our hearts, leaders may become victimized by their own schemes and imaginations. "God shapes the heart of the leader through the call. This call is a divinely orchestrated setting apart of the leader for some special task. God's part of the call dynamic is to initiate, guide, position and intervene. The leader's part of the call drama is to hear, respond, search and order or re-order life" (McNeal 2000, p. 95).

Times are changing and the cultural climatic is adapting in ways that will place greater importance on emerging Kingdom leaders. According to McNeal, pseudo-spiritual leaders will no longer float among Christians unidentified.

> There may have been a day when a spiritual leader without a call could serve in call-like capacities or with call expectations. This will become increasingly difficult to pull off, especially with the demands placed on those who are being called into Christian

leadership in the 21st century. The call will no longer automatically command the respect it once did in the church culture. It will involve more than service; it will exact a sacrifice. The call of God in the days ahead will not grant a person automatic privilege or power but rather potential persecution and certain pain … The point is this; it is tough enough to serve as a Christian leader with a call. Without it, the choice constitutes cruel and unusual self-punishment (McNeal 2000, p. 99).

Borrowing from a Western perspective of separation between the secular and sacred activities of life, different courses of development become visible. Leadership in the body of Christ is on a different trajectory and far more encompassing than the secular course. The center of development is the heart of the leader with the final formation being shaped in the image of Christ. This shaping begins with an understanding of a divine call and materializes in the actualization of leadership roles marked by transformational strategies.

Transformational Leadership

> Leadership in the body of Christ is on a different trajectory and far more encompassing than the secular course.

Ministry gifts to the church as in apostles, prophets, pastors, teachers and evangelists (Ephesians 4:11-12) have exercised leadership in various ways. Whereas some have lead by the sheer force of their personality, otherwise described as charisma, others may have led from the respect that their positions provide. In recent years scholars and researchers have begun to categorize leadership styles and activities. One such style of leadership that has gained approval in several different venues is transformational leadership.

A discussion of transformational leadership, particularly among secular entities, begins with James Burns, a political scientist, who developed his model based on Weber's (1947) work on charismatic leaders. Burns was seeking to differentiate between transactional and charismatic styles of leadership. Burns coined the term transformational because he felt that the term charismatic did not accurately characterize the behavior that was being identified. "Burns described some politicians as 'heroic' (he believed that the term charisma had lost its meaning), in that 'leaders and followers raise one another to higher levels of morality and motivation'. He believed that by engaging the followers' higher needs, transformational leaders move followers beyond their self-interest to work for the greater good and, that as they do so, they become self-actualizing and become leaders themselves" (Alimo-Metcalfe and Alban-Metcalfe 2001, p. 1).

Applications of transformational leadership are diverse, however, the general understanding of a transformational leader is one who, "Focuses on modifying and revising followers' beliefs to generate acceptance of organizational goals and to secure followers' commitment toward the realization of organizational vision. The leader's task is to present followers with the organization's vision and then encourage them to incorporate this vision into their value systems and to put the organization before their own self-interest" (Grundstein-Amado and Rivka 1999, p. 1). Transformational leadership is a style that has captured the respect of the public and private sector. Whether the venue is international entities, educational systems, sports or public health administration, transformational leadership results in change that is grounded in biblical principles.

Business and Politics

The call has been sounded in secular circles for a new approach in executing leadership. The preferred approach is transformational. In 2001, a joint conference on business and politics was held between the United States and Japan where the focus was on leadership issues appropriated in both countries. Representatives David M. Abshire, president of the Center for the Study of the Presidency, and Dr. Inamori from Japan, recognizing the place of significance the countries hold in world business and politics, presented recommendations for a move away from transactional leadership and towards transformational leadership. In a speech on the topic, Abshire stated, "My argument today is that the leadership challenge to Japan, as indeed it is to the United States, as I shall later argue, is to develop a new wave of transformational leadership. Second, both of us should develop transforming ways in which the two largest economic powers can better work together for global economic health and security" (Abshire 2001, p. 1).

World leaders charged with the responsibility to analyze the long-term impact of daily leadership skills upon global concerns seem to understand that transformational leadership is empowering to the organization and those connected to it. Transformational leaders are the truest form of teachers because they show the masses how to think beyond the parameters of self-interest.

Education

The concept of transformational leadership is more than a theory; it is a flexible approach that has been adapted for specialized settings. Educators in multicultural settings are convinced that this approach to leadership has the ability to produce quality life throughout the educational process. "Transformational leadership is philosophically and functionally compatible with a principal's efforts at developing a multicultural learning community. Applying his [Burns'] formulations to a school setting, the exercise of such leadership by the principal would serve to raise levels of motivation and morality for both the administrator and staff. A stimulus that can propel and sustain efforts at building an effective multicultural organization is rooted in mutual support in the pursuit of a common purpose, a defining characteristic of transformational leadership (Jason 2000, p. 1).

Intercollegiate Sports

The work of ministry is taxing on the emotional, physical, psychological and social aspects of those called to do this life impacting work. Quality of life becomes an issue for the ministers who may find themselves feeling unappreciated, exhausted and financially inadequately compensated. Leading God's people as a transformational leader creates an atmosphere that counteracts many of these quality life issues. Researchers in the intercollegiate sports setting discovered the positive effects of transformational leadership in that environment, especially as it related to job satisfaction.

> This study has important implications for practitioners and researchers in sport settings. From a practical standpoint, the results suggest the need for more transformational leaders in sport settings. Specifically, since job satisfaction has been shown to be positively related with high subordinates' performance, low job turnover, low absenteeism and higher productivity, athletic directors who are transformational will make a significant difference in terms of their organization's performance and effectiveness. Further, since transformational leaders can be trained (Bass 1990), training athletic directors and sport administrators to be transformational leaders should be the top priority of sport organizations. In addition, sport organizations should screen candidates for administrative positions on the basis of their potential to be transformational leaders. From a theoretical standpoint, this study has provided evidence of the applicability of the transformational leadership theory in sport settings. Specifically, this study has shown that transformational leaders exist not only in business organizations but also in intercollegiate athletic settings (Yusof 1998, p. 1).

Public Health

Job satisfaction and leadership turnover are two occurrences that can impact the organizational structure, performance quality and the individual worker. Ministry leaders are not excluded from these problems and churches infected by this are finding that the correlation between dissatisfied pastors and leadership turnover can impede the ministry's vision significantly. The issue at hand is one of total quality for those providing ministry services and for those receiving the ministry services.

Health care organizations that are concerned with total quality management and are striving to provide world-class services, have found a method of leadership that has proven results in dealing with these issues. Their chosen solution is the use of transformational leadership implemented by head nurses. In a study conducted to discover the benefits of transformational leadership the following conclusions were made.

> Transformational values and competencies will become critically important by the year 2001 if we are to achieve a health system that fosters community well-being and basic care for all, financed through a combined public/ private partnership that is cost effective and uses treatments that unite body, mind and spirit. Nurses, by virtue of their knowledge, professional status and numbers, are in an excellent position to influence the use of transformational strategies in many health-care organizations throughout the world.

> World-class health-care organizations driven by transformational leaders will create a corporate culture that allows all workers to make a contribution, not just a living, where learning will be emphasized over security and personal responsibility over control.

> The study results indicated that head nurses
> with high transformational scores were more
> likely to have staff nurses with higher job
> satisfaction scores and a longer association
> with their staff nurses than transactional-type
> head nurse leaders (an exchange of reward for
> effort) (Trofino 2000, p. 1).

The use of transformational leadership in secular enterprises demonstrates an awareness of its relevance and potential for effectiveness. This form of leadership translates many biblical principles into concrete actions. It is encouraging to see the variety of professions that have embraced biblical teachings in their management styles, even though alternative language is used in descriptions.

In this chapter the process of development was examined from the perspective of popular notions among the secular environment and sacred traditions. Mentoring was identified and defined as one process of developing. In its completeness, Christian mentors are committed persons who give mutually through experience with the goal of sharing God's resources for Kingdom purposes. A second development concept termed coaching has gained popular appeal. Coaching seeks to nurture untapped human strength and those who offer themselves as coaches do so at a negotiated market price. The motivation is that of career selection as a human service professional and not necessarily functioning in direct response to a divine call from God.

The preferred process of development for Kingdom leaders is accomplished as God shapes and reshapes the heart towards the image of Christ. The value of this particular form of development will become more evident as 21st century expectations exact a great level of competence upon Kingdom leaders.

Leadership styles such as charismatic and transactional are being challenged by transforma-tional strategies. Transformation-al leadership should be the goal within the Kingdom of God as women and men emerge into po-sition. The benefit of transforma-tional strategies has been studied,

As organizations that are driven by profit and loss statements have applied a biblically-based management practice, the church also needs to awaken and reevaluate its current state of affairs.

proven and accepted in a variety of settings to include busi-ness, education, sports and health care.

Development of leaders is not a casual activity if the organization is concerned for its constituents and the overall quality of its future. As organizations that are driven by profit and loss statements have applied a biblically based management practice, the church so too needs to awaken and reevaluate its current state of affairs.

CHAPTER 7

Development of The
Mentoring Model

*Do your best to present yourself to God as one
approved by him, a worker who has no need to be
ashamed, rightly explaining the word of truth
(2 Tim. 2:15).*

S olid ideas are based in research and investigation,
not just theory. For this reason biblical, historical
and theological perspectives have been researched
in order to lay the foundation for the development of a
clergy-mentoring model. Additional structural support has
been provided as a result of investigating contemporary

literature written on practices that have direct impact upon the necessity and implementation of a clergy-mentoring model. The conclusions from all sources are unanimous; a need exists for clergy to be developed as they discern the call, train and become elevated into positions of leadership. In this chapter you are provided insight into the process that was followed for the development and evaluation of the clergy-mentoring model.

How It Came To Be

Development of the model was a slow process that began during initial conversations conducted with clergy peers. Through these conversations, areas of need and problem identification started to filter into the design process. Along each step of the journey, I reserved time for prayer and reflection upon the wisdom that had been shared by the participants and peers. Once the interview process was completed and the tapes were replayed, I presented my findings to the Lord in prayer and then waited for the Lord to enlighten my understanding.

Little by little, the Holy Spirit began to speak wisdom to my spirit about how to proceed with the model design. It became apparent that there is no one approach to meet the needs created by a lack of mentoring. The Mentoring Model needed a design that produces an atmosphere, which repeatedly communicates the necessity and intentional life of mentoring. This model allows for flexibility in connecting with prospective mentors and apprentices. The model is empowering because involvement is not imposed, but is collaborative and selective. In some instances, the model functions as a support system, where in other instances it is a catalyst.

Equipped with insight from the Lord, the conclusions and interpretations are examined here. Goals have been prioritized according to significance, leading with the most significant findings.

Evaluator's Profile

Given the nature of my methodology, soliciting the reflective memories of clergy leaders, I realized that it would be paramount for my participant search to be couched, directed and assessed in prayer. I regularly prayed the following prayer, "Lord, please grant me access to the schedule, heart and memories of those clergy who have the wisdom, in this area, that will provide the Kingdom with the direction you desire for us to follow". I found this prayer to be an encouraging reminder when contact and coordination with clergy became unreasonable.

The participants interviewed represented seven streams of Protestant denominations. The mentor's pastoral exposure ranged from a congregational membership of 180 for the smallest to in excess of 12,000 for the largest. During their tenure of pastoral ministry, five of the mentors have witnessed an explosion of growth within the membership. The remainder of the mentors and apprentices have nurtured existing congregations, resulting in a steady increase in the depth of their ministry.

Although each of the mentors have maximized the availability of their weekly schedules, most of them have dedicated the time to mentor or father/mother more than

20 emerging Kingdom leaders. These women and men who serve as mentors do so out of a great sense of gratitude and connection to God. One of the mentors shared that he had never been blessed to have the wisdom of a mentor during his entrance into ministry. As a result of this awful experience, he made a vow to God that he would not allow that travesty to happen to those whom were under his influence.

The gender mix among evaluators represented a majority (67 percent) male population and minority (33 percent) female. The ethnic mix, as much as can be determined, included a small percentage (17 percent) of non African-American and the balance being African-Americans. The ethnic information was obtained when evaluators chose to include their names on the evaluation survey. This was an option that many chose not to exercise.

The majority of the evaluators were between 30-50 years of age with the greater percentage (42 percent) in the 30s. With one exception, the evaluators were ordained clergy.

The highest percentage of evaluators (25 percent) have been in ministry for 11-16 years. For the remainder of evaluators, a smooth distribution (17 percent) from one to 10 years and more than 29 years (17 percent) exists. As the evaluators entered ministry it appears that they shortly thereafter began to serve as mentors.

The majority (75 percent) of evaluators have served as a mentor for less than 16 years (see Figure 1).

Figure 1. Years as a Mentor

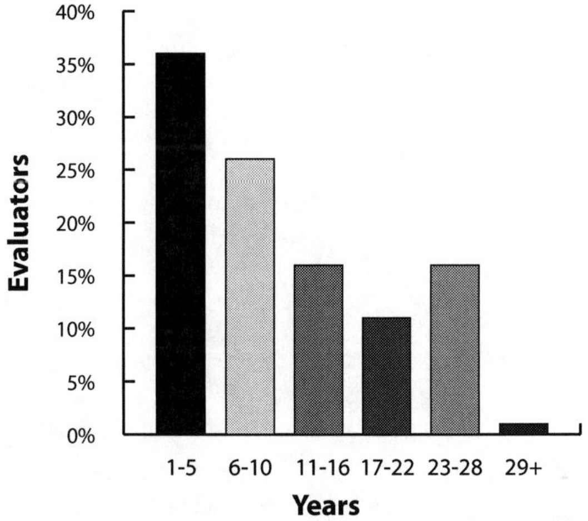

Mentoring relationships among many (71 percent) evaluators tended to be short term, lasting less than three years. While not all evaluators provided reasons for the short terms, those who did cited leadership placement for the apprentice, change in expectations, disagreements and relocation as factors.

When reflecting upon their previous experience of serving as an apprentice, evaluators indicated that several clergy had mentored them in their journey towards leadership. It appears that the evaluators had benefited from multiple, informal mentoring relationships with a small group (19 percent) identifying the presence of more than 29 mentors influencing their development. Those leaders having more than 29 mentors have also been in ministry for more than 30 years.

The concept of mentoring has taken residence within the evaluators. Evidence of this is seen in their involvement with emerging leaders with an impressive amount (52 percent) having personally mentored 1-10 clergypersons (see Figure 2).

Figure 2.   Apprentices Mentored by Evaluators

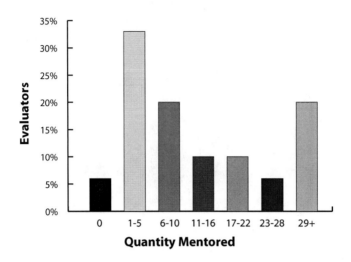

One evaluator with less than five years of ministry experience, and the absence of a previous mentoring experience, was the one exception to this finding and had never mentored anyone in ministry.

Whether formally or informally, local congregations were involved in the mentoring experience for the majority (58 percent) of the evaluators. Evaluators did not describe the particularities of congregational involvement.

Let's Talk About the Model

The model designed from this research is multifaceted in that it has training, marketing, enlightening and challenging components combined to create an interdependent process. As a result, each component of the model was examined as a separate unit and not all of the components were designed to address each goal. Although each component was examined as a separate unit, the results from one unit often impact other units.

For example, the Conference and the Broadcast Units have been designed to raise the level of consciousness as it relates to mentoring and to persuade leaders to participate in the mentoring process. The Clergy Mentoring Institute (CMI) is the vehicle for leaders to identify God's call upon apprentices, intentionally mentor them and to do so in a manner that is consistent with the example set by Jesus. Likewise, the Peer Mentoring Unit facilitates the Jesus model of mentoring because it fosters relationship among peers, as Jesus did with the disciples.

Overall the goals of The Mentoring Model are as follows:

- Goal one — help leaders identify God's calling upon apprentices.
- Goal two — help leaders implement methods to mentor apprentices.
- Goal three — help leaders discern when it is time to elevate their apprentice into leadership.
- Goal four — persuade leaders to value and participate in a mentoring/apprentice process.
- Goal five — help leaders accept their responsibility in the training of their ministerial staff.
- Goal six — the model would be based primarily in the mentor-teacher training modeled by Jesus.

THE CLERGY MENTORING INSTITUTE ™

Modeled After Jesus

The intensive training unit designed in this model was most successful in meeting goal number six; a mentor-teacher training modeled by Jesus. The CMI is designed as a one-year learning incubator that convenes quarterly for a period of one week. The CMI is a catalyst for structuring the process; therefore mentors and apprentices would be expected to continue their relationship beyond the one-year institute.

Figure 3. One-Year Duration of Training Unit

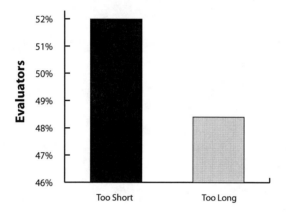

The greatest challenge confronting the CMI is the ability to address time considerations. Admittedly this requires a genuine commitment on behalf of all involved. When asked for reasons that clergy would not participate in the training unit; time and insecurity were the leading obstacles. The majority of the evaluators (52 percent) believed the one-year duration was adequate but bordered on too short (see Figure 3), however the five-day frequency was a point of greatest concern. Results were divided between too long (61 percent) and too short (39 percent) (see Figure 4).

Without argument, intentional mentoring demands bountiful amounts of time commitment, yet there are those

Figure 4. Five-Day Frequency of Training Sessions

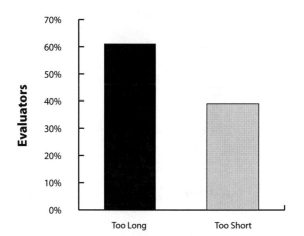

exceptional clergy who carve out the time in order to fulfill this divine calling.

Participation in the CMI sessions requires both parties in the set to be present for each quarterly gathering. Like the relationship between Jesus and the disciples, this joint learning experience provides opportunities for bonding. The evaluators also believed in the value of joint learning with an overwhelming majority (63 percent) in favor of unified training. Only one evaluator found absolutely no value in joint learning (see Figure 5).

A word needs to be said concerning the method of joining the mentor and apprentice. This model is not designed to pair groups of clergy together. The model is designed to facilitate a mentoring relationship that was formed in an independent context. This approach accounts for how and why clergy will participate in the training. For example, if an apprentice who desires to participate in the training unit approaches a mentor, with an extremely busy

Figure 5.   Joint Participation

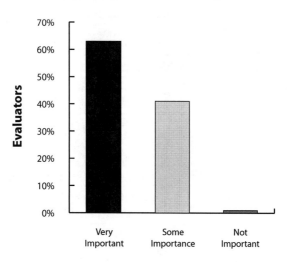

schedule, and asks them to join in the training, a strong possibility exists that the mentor will grant the request. Although time and inconvenience are factors, granting the request becomes a function of love towards the apprentice.

Valuing the Process

Persuading professional clergy to value and partici-pate in a mentor/apprentice process was the second great-est accomplishment. Evaluators were asked to describe ways that the training unit would positively impact the Black church and the Kingdom of God. Although this project is not restricted by ethnicity, gender or denomination, evalu-ators were asked to assess the benefits to the Black church. The reason for this assessment question relates the cultural context of how African-American people "do" church and the social implications that are particular to this context. The diversity of answers demonstrated a felt value in the need for intentional training and the particular benefits clergy would be able to realize upon participation in the model. Some of the strongest felt benefits include intentional leadership development, resources and training avail-

Figure 6. Prevailing Impacts for the Black Church

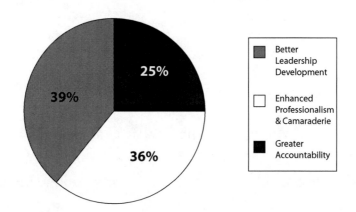

able for mentors, generational learning, enhanced professionalism and camraderie among clergy (see Figure 6).

The impact of intensive training for the Kingdom of God was equally encouraging. Some of the strongest felt benefits included; creating balance and diversity between old and young leaders, break down cultural and denominational barriers and leadership identification (see Figure 7). One evaluator stated that it is a long overdue model for ministry.

Without exception, clergy communicated the obvious need and desire for intentional mentoring within the profession, however gauging the willingness of clergy to actually participate in the process was another issue. Opinions among evaluators communicated a moderate willingness (55 percent) on behalf of clergy to participate in the

Figure 7. Prevailing Impacts in the Kingdom of God

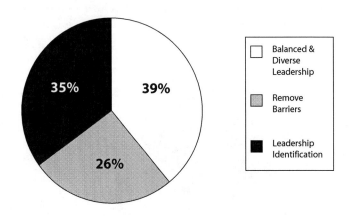

training. Willingness to participate as a mentor comes from a belief in the value of giving back to the community or profession. This willingness finds competition with the demands of time and personal exposure that are by-products of mentoring. However evaluators strongly believed (59 percent) there is likelihood that after participating in the training unit, clergy would be persuaded to value the mentor/apprentice process. These statistics seem to suggest a level of confidence in the training unit. It also communicates the hope that once exposed, clergy will see God's anointing in this area of work.

Identifying God's Call

Helping professional clergy leaders identify God's calling upon clergy apprentices was the third achievable goal possible through the training unit. The ministry emphasis among some groups of pastors appears to be the fulfillment of their vision. Those who come within their influence, especially persons with obvious gifts and talents, are seen primarily as agents to help them in their quest. Rare is the clergy leader who is intentional about discerning God's activity in another's life simply for the purpose of developing that person into leadership. One of the evaluators stated simply that clergy do not have a vision for anything that is not immediately beneficial to their own congregations. In a word, clergy leaders are disinterested in developing emerging leaders. These are the obstacles confronting a model focused on helping clergy identify God's calling upon the lives of other persons.

Encouragingly, the majority of evaluators (56 percent) communicated confidence that after participating in the training unit, clergy would experience an enormous increase in their ability to discern God's call upon the life of apprentices, and an even greater percentage (62 percent) communicated clergy would experience an enormous increase in their ability to discern when it is time to elevate apprentices into leadership (see Figure 8).

Figure 8. Ability to Discern for Evaluation

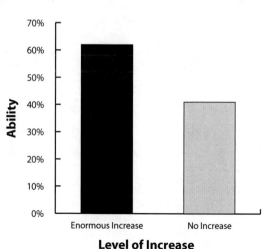

Clearly it is believed that participating in the training unit will shift a leader from being self-interested to Body-interested.

THE CONFERENCE UNIT

Accept Responsibility

The Conference Unit takes advantage of a strategic opportunity to meet clergy and potential clergy. In short, it is a marketing vehicle for the practice of intentional mentoring.

Figure 9. Possible Impact of the Conference Unit

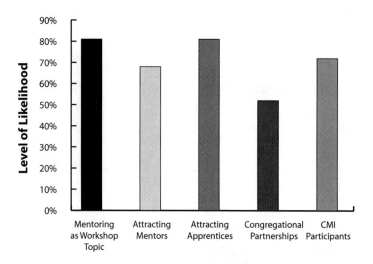

Evaluators were sensitive to the availability of leadership conferences hosted each year by broad constituencies in the Kingdom. The encouraging response was that most (79 percent) of the evaluators believed that this arena would be very valuable for attracting apprentices. The Conference Unit would also be very valuable for attracting mentors accordin to many (66 percent) of the evaluators (see Figure 9).

The success of the Conference Unit is based upon collaborative relationships with churches, ministries and theological institutions that host leadership conferences. The majority of evaluators (79 percent) felt strongly that these organizations would be very willing to include clergy mentoring as a workshop among their topics.

As previously stated, the Mentoring Model contains interdependent units that address targeted populations. The Conference Unit proves to be the best component of the model to raise the level of consciousness of clergy as it relates to the need for intentional mentoring. The impact of the Conference Unit is also seen on the CMI, wherein half (50 percent) of the evaluators believed that it would be very valuable for gaining congregational partnerships. A majority (70 percent) also believed it would be a very effective arena for canvassing participants for the CMI.

THE BROADCAST UNIT

The Broadcast Unit is like net fishing. The strategy is to minister the gospel of mentoring by capturing the attention of a massive group. Stated another way, it is a persuasive voice that seeks to address goal numbers four and five — persuade clergy to accept their responsibility in the training of their ministerial staff.

Although many evaluators (more than 52 percent) indicated favorable benefits of the Broadcast Unit, it was clear that their confidence in radio ministries is not compelling. Research information that demonstrates usage patterns for Christian radio ministries was obtained prior to formulating the survey questions. Because of the compelling data that indicates usage levels for Christian radio to be extremely positive, it never occurred to me to ask narrative questions in this area. As a result, narrative questions were not directed towards this component of the model, therefore an explanation in this area would only be speculation on behalf of the researcher.

In spite of the less than enthusiastic comments made by evaluators, the Broadcast Unit is included here. This decision was based, in part, on the favorable (more than 52 percent) responses (see Figure 10) and on the research data collected by the Barna Research Group.

According to a poll conducted by the Barna Research Group, Christian radio is reaching astounding amounts of

Figure 10. Projected Impact of Broadcast Unit

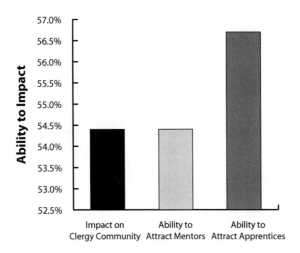

adults each month. In raw numbers, "109 million adults are exposed to Christian radio content" each month (Barna 2002 p. 1). Among these numbers there appears to be a particular population segment that also profiles many of the emerging leaders who may be at the first phase in discerning a divine call.

> The use of Christian media, regardless of type, increased with age until the mid-1970s, at which point usage dropped off somewhat. Women were generally more likely than men to use Christian media, while blacks were substantially more likely than any other ethnic segment to incorporate such media into their life...Residents of the South were much more likely to use any of the Christian media evaluated than were residents of the Northeast and West (Barna 2002, p. 2).

PROJECT PEER MENTORING

The Project Peer Mentoring (PPM) Unit designed in this model was the least successful in meeting any of the intended goals. It was hoped that professional clergy would be receptive to this form of mentoring, especially in light of an apparent absence of elder mentors. I was wrong. Responses from evaluators identified many spiritual and personal benefits of the PPM Unit such as: humility, fresh ideas, reduced sense of isolation and improved listening skills. Evaluators were also convinced (58.92 percent) that clergy would form or participate in peer mentoring groups. Questions were asked to identify reasons why clergy would not participate. Reasons for resistance included; closed-mindedness, fear of transparency and no vision of the possibilities that peer mentoring can provide. Most evaluators (68 percent) felt that the structure was too formal, and many (60 percent) felt that the bi-monthly sessions were too frequent (see Figure 11). It appears clergy are interested in social fellowship with their peers and not necessarily mentoring from their peers. In light of this data, the PPM Unit may be re-conceptualized in the future.

Figure 11. Project Peer Mentoring

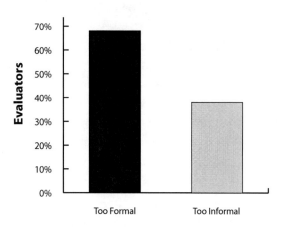

The concept of a clergy-mentoring model has received enormous agreement and verbal support. Participation in the model will prove to be a great challenge as the obstacles of time requirements and reduced personal self-interest become paramount. Earlier, the goals were designed based upon the idea that the model would be one cohesive entity. However, after the research was collected, it became obvious that the need and targeted population was too diverse for one approach and a four-unit approach was developed. The result is a ministry model directed towards the intentional development of clergy leadership.

Some aspects of the model will have to be re-conceptualized before implementation. Other portions of the model, such as the Conference Unit have already begun as the Lord has been opening doors of opportunity for me to teach and preach on this very topic of leadership. In either case, partnerships with others in ministry will become vitally important. Hope exists that as people become acquainted with the vision, that they will use their influence to make implementation possible. Collaborative relationships have been and will continue to be the key for acceptance. All it takes is someone willing to make a telephone call to their peer and say, "I know this anointed preacher who has a vision for clergy mentoring. I recommend that you invite her to participate in the next leadership conference that you host". In a sense, the Clergy Mentoring Model needs a mentor.

CHAPTER 8

Moved To Mentor

*I*f *you put these instructions before the brothers and sisters, you will be a good servant of Christ Jesus, nourished on the words of the faith and of the sound teaching that you have followed.... These are the things you must insist on and teach. Let no one despise your youth, but set the believers an example in speech and conduct, in love, in faith, in purity. Until I arrive, give attention to the public reading of scripture, to exhorting, to teaching. Do not neglect the gift that is in you, which was given to you through prophecy with the laying on of hands by the council of elders. Put these things into practice, devote yourself to them, so that all may see your progress. Pay close attention to yourself and to your teaching;*

*continue in these things, for in doing this you will
save both yourself and your hearers (1Timothy
4:6, 11-16).*

Good advice for doing ministry... putting what
you've been taught into practice. Line upon line, precept
upon precept I've invited you, the reader to see the problem, hear the thoughts of others concerning the problem
and even introduced a path out of this barren land. Now
let us come and reflect on what has been for some a challenge and/or confrontational proposal of action; an effective process for professional clergy to methodically and intentionally identify, mentor and elevate clergy apprentices
into transformational leadership?

Clergy are interested in engaging in a discussion on
the topic of mentoring but unless there is a clearly identified
personal gain, a directive from ecclesiastical superiors, or
a strong suggestion from a person of influence to become
involved, a significant contingent of clergy leaders are not
likely to devote the time to intentional mentoring. In spite
of these constraints this is what we've come to know about
the need for this Mentoring Model.

Knowing How

Equipping clergy leaders to become proficient mentors of other clergy attributes a sense of desire and willingness onto elder leaders. Christians posses a utopian ideal
that fellow citizens, and especially leaders, have humbled
their own personal ambitions and are intent on doing what
is best for the Kingdom. If clergy are not intentionally men-

toring other clergy, and many are not, a utopian analysis may conclude that it is not happening simply because the leaders do not know how to carry forth the task. Thus, the need for the development of a model to "teach" clergy how to do what they apparently do not know how to do. One common saying, people who know better will do better, makes this point. But will they? Sadly, there are clergy who have witnessed the need and effects of mentoring but have excused themselves out of the arena of responsibility.

As I reflect on what I've learned about equipping clergy leaders to be mentors, it is first that facts and intellectual knowledge are the least valuable tools. Professional clergy are smart people who have studied the word of God in an organized fashion. Many have seen the demonstration of the Holy Spirit at work in their life and ministry. Most have an

People who know better will do better.

ongoing relationship with Christ Jesus. Their minds are full of facts and knowledge, but mentoring moves far past these compartments. The ministry has remnants of a caste system. People have reservations when it comes to living connectedly with those of like callings. I have learned that a facilitated environment, built upon consistency, clarity and commitment will move those who are willing into the life of clergy mentoring. For those who know better but excuse themselves from doing better, there remains the hope that they will humble themselves, pray and turn from their wicked ways. When that turning takes place, it will be good to have a ministry that is dedicated to this form of restoration.

The Problem of Time

I once heard an elder pastor say that preaching grows the congregation, not administration, but as the congregation grows then the pastor is needed to devote more time to administration. In the end, less time is spent on studying the word and consequently preaching suffers and ultimately the congregation begins to decline in size and depth. The problem is one of time. Clergy are bombarded with expectations that have been placed upon them. The needs of the people are constant, the needs of the family are often overshadowed and the need for personal attention is many times neglected.

In addition to the demands of clergy life are the instances of poor task-management skills, lack of delegation and micro-management. There just doesn't seem to be enough time for God's leaders to do the work assigned to their hands. Of course, one wonders if God has assigned much of the work that leaders are doing or did they self-initiate these roles. In the words of Bishop Don Mears of Evangel Church in Bowie, Maryland, "All the devil has to do is give you a good idea to destroy your ministry and make you ineffective in the Kingdom".

Mentoring requires bountiful amounts of time, especially where there is a desire to be intentional and relational. There are clergy who seldom take vacations, educational sabbaticals or spiritual retreats. In these instances, when would someone become available to attend a training session no matter the length of the session? At first glimpse, the prospects appear discouraging. I recognize the problem, yet I have known extremely busy and obligated clergy who make the time for intentional mentoring. Each year clergy have enrolled in doctorate programs, masters programs and continued education that will have time requirements similar to the intensive training designed in this mentoring project. Yet they find and/or make time to fulfill their personal goal of development. Narrow is the path that has been treaded out by mentors because few, very few, heed the call. Of course there is the option of reducing the frequency and length of each training session but such an approach disregards the objective as a whole by assuming that all of mentoring takes place during the training. The training sessions are periods of consecration for the work that takes place on location.

New Relationships

The final question on the survey asked if the evaluator would be willing to mentor me as I fulfill the call God has placed upon my life. The majority said they would be very willing, yet only one initiated any communication with me to ascertain the progress of my studies or to offer encouragement. I am reminded of my years spent working in professional sales. We were taught that when prospecting for new clients, for every 10 persons we met as prospects, only one person would ultimately become a client. It appears that the statistics also hold true when building relationships in the Kingdom.

Hard Realities

This book was written before I became a pastor. As a result of not having ever served as a pastor, I faced some harsh and hard realities when pondering how my research would be implemented. May I say out loud what all of us know? If one is not a pastor, then the clergy community, especially pastors, do not give strong attention to your voice; generally speaking of course. Towards the end of my doctoral studies I made the untimely mistake of sharing my vision with one of our denominational bishops, whose identify will remain concealed. The response I received was... well I'll let you judge for yourself! This is what the bishop said, "Reverend, who is going to listen to you? You've never pastored a church. By what authority do you speak? You need to pastor before you start trying to tell pastors what they should be doing."

Wow, okay... thank you for your support! Even though the tone was condescending and the words cutting, I could not disregard the content of the message. Persons who think like this particular bishop say, in effect, that unless one has served as a pastor their experiences count for very little. Without taking respect and honor away from the office of pastor, I strongly believe that God uses more than one position to edify the body of Christ. Well, I remained steadfast and did not succumb to discouraging comments like these. I was and am not a blank sheet of paper that only the role of pastor can write upon, and thus validate the anointing on my life, despite the fact that I currently serve as a pastor. The experiences God has given me are meaningful and valuable to the Kingdom. For all who cannot or will not appreciate this, I will shake the dust off my feet and keep pressing forward. Instead I did what I always do when

May I say out loud what all of us know?

there is a mountain in my path; I prayed. I have been called to serve in this capacity and of this I am clear. God's calling and anointing is upon my life, but many people look for position before they look for God's presence. Without the position of pastor, the results of my survey and informal discussions told me that those for whom I have been called to help may not hear or listen to my voice. These facts alone suggest that this model would equate to nothing more than a couple hundred words printed on crisp white paper. But GOD!

In *This is My Story; Testimonies and Sermons of Black Women In Ministry* I had the blessed opportunity to share my testimony about moving from the pew into the pulpit. In this testimony I share how God changed the circumstances of my life by placing me into the role of a pastor. If being a pastor was the necessary element to have this work heard … don't make me preach about how God is able to perfect that which concerns you!

During this project God spoke revelation to me several times communicating the struggle between the flesh and the spirit. The hard realities of our circumstances always point to the analysis of physical eyes but when seen through the spirit our heart becomes encouraged. God will make exceptions where necessary. God will provide opportunities where they are expedient. This calling is spirit and I have received it as such. I always believed that somewhere, somehow, one day God would place all things in order so that this calling would be established. I found myself revisiting the words of my beloved mentor; Rev. Dr. Samuel Dewitt Proctor, when he would remind me that all I needed was more time. In time God would work it all out.

Final Thoughts

A large group (54 percent) of evaluators, of which were between 40-69 years of age believed that few (less than four percent) of their counterparts (in age) would submit themselves as apprentices in a training experience (see Figure 12). This conclusion is particularly interesting in light of the occurrences of persons who enter ministry as a second career or later in life. Second career ministers are much more likely to fit within the age bracket that the evaluators discounted as potential apprentice participants.

Figure 12. Average Age of Apprentices

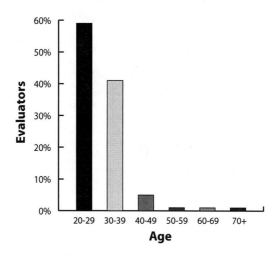

Evaluators also did not believe that anyone aged in their 20s or 70s would or could serve as mentors (see Figure 13). The conclusion drawn from this response is that youthful clergy possess very little, if any, wisdom that would be beneficial for developing emerging Kingdom leaders. Oddly enough, many clergy within this age bracket find

Figure 13. Average Age of Mentors

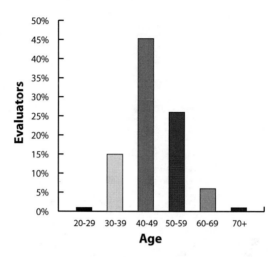

themselves serving various denominations as senior pastors, a responsibility for which wisdom is a chief element. For those clergy 70 years and beyond, perhaps it is assumed that the time commitment for mentoring may be too demanding, although in some denominations persons within this age bracket are often retired and may have more time available. However that leads to the question of relevance and whether clergy beyond 70 years of age are able to remain current/relevant in vision, method and mission.

The implication for Kingdom leadership is sobering. The perception is that with youth comes a low degree of wisdom and with age comes a low degree of relevance or open-mindedness. It also appears that clergy experience their zenith while in their 40s. This is particularly alarming for congregational bodies under ecclesiastical supervision. A common attitude, especially in the AMEC, is that everyone starts ministry at the "bottom". The "bottom" describes congregations that have minimal resources;

people and facilities and major obstacles; lack of vision and unwillingness. A neophyte pastor could spend a decade or more in this type of situation. Sexism in the church makes the prospects even more dismal for female clergy. The hope is that denominational authorities will become progressive thinkers and break from traditional paradigms that handicap the church.

The other sobering implication addresses the condition of denominations whose top leadership is comprised of persons over 65 years of age. In some denominations bishops continue to pastor a local congregation, which has the potential of keeping them in touch (relevant) with the people they serve. But then there are other denominations that remove bishops from congregational life and place them strictly in supervisory roles. As these leaders continue to age, it becomes challenging for their methods, message and mission to remain relevant. These insights suggest that congregational bodies should re-evaluate leadership profiles and consider including younger clergy for influential positions.

Personal Goals

I do not desire to present a completely bleak description of my ministry. Being resourceful when it comes to gaining insight and wisdom has created collegial bonds for which I passionately value. However, many of my experiences in ministry have been wrought with mismanagement, indifference and intentional misdirection from some clergy who exercised direct pastoral authority, and other clergy who had indirect power over my ministerial development.

I have never fully understood why this has been the case and I became concerned that others were living the same nightmare. Therefore I set personal goals for this project that addressed limited as well as expansive circles within the Kingdom of God as I attempted to find meaning in my journey. They were:

- Goal one — demonstrate the ministry of providing an apprentice relationship whenever the situation arises.
- Goal two — learn to equip clergy leaders to become proficient in mentoring clergy apprentices.
- Goal three — develop relationships with clergy leaders outside of my present denominational and cultural context so that Sharing Faith Ministries will have an avenue of influence.
- Goal four — gain new meaning into my own journey in clergy leadership development.

Personal Findings

Goal two was the most successful of all personal goals. The literary research was very helpful in constructing the model; however, the individual interviews proved to be as valuable as precious gemstones. Clergy were transparent in their reflections which allowed wisdom, otherwise unattainable, and presently not documented, to be gathered. Combining current research with sage wisdom has gifted me with revelation, information and inspiration to help clergy become proficient in mentoring emerging clergy leaders.

Goal three was the next attainable goal. One of the survey questions pointedly asked evaluators if they would be willing to intentionally mentor me as I seek to fulfill the call of ministry God has placed upon my life. The results were encouraging with most (75percent) of the responses stating a strong willingness. Beyond the survey measurement was the sense of connection that I felt along the research journey. Clergy outside of my gender, ethnicity and denominational affiliation were eager to dialogue with me and to provide assistance in the future implementation of the model.

I do believe the guiding force in this area was a discerning word from God that said, "Listen to new voices." In this directive I understood God to mean that I should be open to the voice of clergy that I have not been previously exposed. Responding to God's directive, I intentionally sought an audience with educators, pastors and preachers with whom I did not have any connection. In response to the foundational prayer of this research, God gave me access to "new voices" in the Kingdom.

The opportunity to mentor others has become available to a significant degree as I now serve on the AMEC Michigan Annual Conference Board of Examiners as the Chair of First Year Studies. This is the organization within our denomination entrusted with the responsibility to monitor the academic and to some extent, spiritual readiness of emerging clergy. My students might tell you that I am passionate about their progress, so much so that whenever possible I set the barr (excuse the pun) very high. Peers have affirmed God's calling and anointing upon my life and they have become interested/willing to accept me as a mentor. Of course there are those peers for whom I've felt as if I serve informally as a mentor, given the frequency that they call for advice (disguised as general conversation) and the regularity in which they implement my "comments".

I have gained new meaning into my own journey in

clergy leadership development, but not full understanding. In this respect I am reminded that in this life, not all things are fully revealed. The meaning that I have gained points mostly to the impact that implementing this model will have on the Kingdom of God. Through my experiences I have been molded with compassion for others growing in their calling. This quality alone can make a difference in the way leaders are developed.

> Will the fathers and mothers give their hearts towards spiritual nurture of God's leaders?

Last Words

The Kingdom of God needs transformational leaders and these leaders need mentors. Transformational leadership is grounded in biblical foundations, and to the surprise of some, organizations that are not necessarily Christian are embracing these foundations. Not all businesses and organizations have opted for the life of transformational leadership, but those that have are cheering the concept. This begs the question as to why the church, guardians of the foundations, seems to be many decades behind in applying transformational leadership. If the church were profit-driven like corporations, would that prove to be the motivating force needed to implement mentoring among leadership? Clearly the clergy has issues.

Will the fathers and mothers give their hearts towards spiritual nurture of God's leaders? The need is present but determining the desire within the workers is difficult. I have desired to help others fulfill God's call upon their lives and out of this desire emerged a model of ministry. In so many ways I feel like Moses when he expressed certainty that Pharaoh would not listen to him. But like Moses, it has been more important to me to please God than to withdraw in the face of obstacles. I wish I could say that I know the end of this matter. All I do know is that this is God's work and that I have been called to perform it.

My personal growth during this process has traveled along every end of the scale. Some days I have experienced a zealous excitement, other days I wondered if my pursuit was in vain. All of these expressions are part of the journey that I have been privileged to travel. Rejection is powerful and when viewed properly it can propel you into your destiny. This is the most valuable lesson I have learned. If I had never received another mentor during my journey in ministry, I would forever be shaped by the few years that Rev. Dr. Samuel DeWitt Proctor invested in my growth. Dr. Proctor would occassionaly say to me, "You just need time". To you my sisters and brothers I say, REDEEM THE TIME.

CHAPTER 9

The Clergy Mentoring Model

The model designed from this research includes several strategies for inspiring participation and disseminating the biblical, theological and historical information under girding clergy apprenticeship. The primary objective of this model is to lead from the heart, wherein the preacher's life experiences become a vibrant part of the model. The flexibility of each strategy shares the spirit of Howard Thurman's testimony as he reflected on methods of learning and development. "I believe that above all else the preacher's life experiences, with his successes and failures, hopes and aspirations, make up the only authentic laboratory in which all his fundamental commitments can be tested" (Thurman 1979, p. 161).

The Mentoring Model contains four strategic units, Intensive Training, Peer Mentoring, Conference Presentation, and Broadcast. The target population for each unit is specific to the existing level of mentor/apprentice interaction, recognized need and willingness to explore, on behalf of the clergy community. Each unit is designed to function independently; however, a subsidiary element of the strategy allows for the Clergy Mentoring Institute to be interconnected with each of the other units.

THE INTENSIVE TRAINING UNIT

> Contact without fellowship tends to be un-
> sympathetic, cold and impersonal, expressing
> itself often in sick or limited forms of ill will;
> ill will easily becomes the ground for suspi-
> cion and hatred. The reverse is also true. Con-
> tact with fellowship is apt to be sympathetic;
> sympathetic understanding often leads to the
> exercise of goodwill.
> (Howard Thurman 1979, p. 147)

The Intensive Training Unit, entitled Clergy Mentoring Institute™ (CMI), is a one-year creative learning incubator that convenes quarterly for the period of one week. The targeted participants for the Clergy Mentoring Institute are sets of mentor-teachers and their apprentices. Participation in CMI sessions requires both parties in the set to be present for each quarterly gathering. Joining the session once it has begun will not be permitted.

CMI sessions will be convened in cities where a local congregation has agreed to work in partnership with

Sharing Faith Ministries. It will be the responsibility of the partner congregation to host a commissioning worship service on the first night of training. The commissioning worship experience will serve to encourage the participants and to affirm for them that members in the body of Christ are appreciative of their dedication. The CMI is described as a creative learning incubator because the structure allows participants to become exposed to academic and experiential wisdom and to practice the lessons learned in this secure environment. CMI is also designed to equip the participants with academic, spiritual and practical wisdom for application in their context between sessions and at the conclusion of the formal training. Materials to be covered include the biblical, historical and theological foundations for mentoring that have been developed in the research of this doctoral paper. Participants will have opportunity to define various aspects of executing the process in their environment to include; relationships, expectations, time considerations and communications. Participants will also be guided to identify areas in need of growth; for example: self-awareness, spiritual disciplines, professional and skills development and discernment. Lastly, participants will spend time visioning the path of ministry that God has prepared for them.

The objective of CMI is for both the mentor and apprentice to have a sound understanding of their responsibilities, a working knowledge of how to actualize the process and to become intentional about their role in each other's lives. The CMI is designed to be experiential in nature. To accomplish this objective, learning activities such as role-playing will be utilized. Participants will be expected to co-minister, during the CMI week session, so that the group will be able to experience the gifts within each member.

The skeletal structure of the CMI session is designed as follows. Monday is set aside for collective fellowship and worship. Participants arrive at the session site; we dine together as a group and then join the partner congregation for worship. Monday night worship is a service of commissioning. Through this worship experience, the participants are focused upon the journey ahead. They consecrate themselves for the divine work of empowering one another through apprenticeship. The participants become aware of the Kingdom impact that their commitment will have upon congregations, as they witness the support of fellow Christians. Participants will also become fully cognizant that their efforts are being supported in prayer and that their success is encouraged.

Tuesday is designed for the participants to understand who we are as mentors and apprentices. Mentors and apprentices will use this day to bring definition to their relationship, as it will be lived out in their particular context. They will discuss expectations each has for the other and for the relationship. Based upon research interviews in this project, the issue of time proved to be a formidable requirement for mentors, therefore participants will also define what will be reasonable time expectations.

Wednesday is designed to understand why we are intentionally involved in the development of leaders. This will be accomplished through studying biblical models of mentoring relationships. Participants will discuss historical models from their own particular traditions. As a whole, the group will also study the theological implications of mentoring and leadership development.

Thursday is designed to understand what we are as leaders in the Kingdom of God. During the interview process mentors admitted that self-awareness turns the tide of training new leaders. Mentors learned that if they were not careful, and self-aware, the process of apprenticeship has the potential of destroying the uniqueness of the apprentice. Each mentor trained their apprentice based upon their own idiosyncrasies. Self-awareness helps the mentor to balance the training and it safeguards the apprentice from adopting issues that were never previously a problem area.

Friday is designed to discern where we are in the process as evolving leaders. The purpose of this project was the development of a model to identify the call to leadership, and to train and elevate women and men into transformational leadership. Friday is the day in which participants discern where they are in the process. Some may be struggling with clarifying the call. Others may be clear about the context of the call to leadership but may need to clarify and plan the type of training that will be needed in order to prepare for transitioning. Finally, there will be those who discern that the season of transition is impending and they need to clarify the requirements for elevation. Each CMI session will conclude as it began with group dining and worship.

Each quarterly convening of CMI will follow the skeletal structure as described, however the emphasis will be customized based upon what was uncovered the previous quarter and the revealed needs of the group. One of the desired goals of the CMI is for participants to be instilled with a commitment towards exponentially producing leaders. To this end, participants will be expected to identify their next apprentice.

THE PEER MENTORING UNIT

> What had I learned about love? One of the central things was that the experience of being understood by another was of primary importance... To find ultimate security in an ultimate vulnerability, this is to be loved. Yet, I had questions. Could this be cultivated in a primary exposure to another human being? Could a climate be established in which it is reasonable and possible for one person to trust another to that extent? Was it possible for such experiences to be programmed?
> (Howard Thurman 1979,p. 146)

The Peer Mentoring unit, entitled Project Peer Mentoring™ (PPM) was birthed out of the reality that clergy who need the advice of seasoned mentors are often unable to obtain an audience with them or establish a relationship. Symbolically speaking, if Moses is unwilling, unavailable or unable to share wisdom with Joshua as he evolves into the leader God has required, then to whom (in addition to the Holy Spirit) can Joshua turn to for encouragement, counsel and accountability? The PPM unit suggests that Joshua can turn to Caleb. Caleb has different ministry responsibilities and less experience than Moses (Joshua 14: 6-14), but Caleb is in touch with Joshua's vision. Caleb's experiences are valuable (Numbers 13) and Caleb is interested in Joshua's success in ministry.

The targeted participants for PPM are clergy and

their spouses (if so interested), who desire to collaborate relationally with other clergy (and their spouses) for the accomplishment of their individual ministries. The participants within PPM must see themselves as Project Managers, and their ministries as Projects. PPM groups will consist of a manageable representative not to exceed seven ministries. PPM groups are held together by a mutual respect for one another based upon the scriptural foundation of the priesthood of all believers (1 Peter 2:9). PPM is the place where leaders in the Kingdom of God realize fellowship in community otherwise known as koinonia. The following is a quote from Robert Schnase that describes the atmosphere for the objectives in PPM.

> We have one another in common... You are present in what I do, and I in what you do. I am part of your ministry, and you are part of mine, because we are both part of Christ. I am accountable for your well-being, as you are for mine. In mutuality, we share one another's burdens, delight in one another's successes, and offer ourselves fully in service to one another. We call one another to greater fullness. It is not you against me, instead of me, under me, or over me. It is you in service to me, and I to you, both of us thereby expressing our service to Christ. (Robert Schnase 1993, p. 101)

PPM groups convene once every other month for a time of fellowship and project reporting. Each project manager is expected to prepare an agenda that covers the items of concern for her/his project. Status reports, personal reflections, requests for ideas or assistance, and any items of concern are verbally presented to the entire group during the dedicated 20 minutes allotted to each project. Continued participation in PPM is voluntary and perpetual. Participants in PPM will be encouraged to identify a member of the clergy who would ultimately become their apprentice at a future time. Once the apprentice has been identified, the mentor will be encouraged to attend the CMI with their apprentice.

THE CONFERENCE UNIT

> A great gift in my life has been the companion who meets me at the gate in any arena where I am called upon to do battle and who with great compassion finds the weak points in my idea or contention without in any way diminishing me (Howard Thurman 1979, 104).

The Conference Unit takes advantage of a strategic opportunity to meet clergy and potential clergy at the gate of spiritual, personal and professional enhancement. Leadership conferences sponsored by churches, ministries and theological institutions have become plentiful. The appearance of these professional development arenas signals a heightened intent toward providing quality leadership in the Kingdom. People want to present their best effort and have come to realize that the call from God is enhanced by continued education and skills development. Often, the format for these conferences includes workshop sessions led by panelists who specialize in a particular area of leadership.

The Conference Unit is a collaborative partnership with churches, ministries and theological institutions that host leadership conferences for ministers. Implementation of this unit is an integral part of my life's work in the area of facilitating clergy to become intentional mentors. The objective of this collaboration is for me, or other ministers associated with Sharing Faith Ministries to serve as a panelist on the topic of intentional mentoring. Presentation of ideas and testimonies from those who have experienced mentoring will be used as a catalyst to awaken attendee's capacity and thoughts in support of mentoring. The targeted participants of The Conference Unit will be conference attendees. The Conference Unit will also serve as a canvassing arena to prospect for clergy mentors to become involved with The Broadcast Unit and to recruit new participants for the CMI and PPM.

THE BROADCAST UNIT

> I never saw Dr. Cross again. When he returned from his sabbatical leave, I received a letter from him saying that he had found my mentor and had completed arrangements for my journey to Europe to study in the fall. We set a date for me to visit him in Rochester, but before I could see him, he died suddenly. He had not shared his plans for me with anyone. I have often wondered where and with whom he had arranged for me to study, but the answer to my question died with him. What difference would it have made? I wonder, but can never know (Howard Thurman 1979, p.61).

The Broadcast Unit is a fishing strategy (John 21:6) to minister the gospel of mentoring by capturing the attention of a massive group. Communication systems have advanced to the point that information on almost any subject is readily available. Ministries, with vision and provision, particularly in the United States, have seized the moment by spreading the gospel of Christ using real time devices such as the Internet, television, and radio. Each medium has benefits and limitations.

For the purposes of this Mentoring Model, it was determined that radio would be the chosen medium with an openness to also include podcasts. Radio ministries remain a popular and affordable mode for spreading the gospel message while podcasts represent cutting edge technology. Using these communication devices takes advantage of a strategic opportunity to dialogue in a non-confrontational venue. A prospective mentor may find it more comfortable to hear about other's experiences before deciding to make space in their life for mentoring. The challenge of mentoring is for the clergy to find value in the process and to own it as their personal mission. Changing ideologies may best be accomplished with steady drops on the same spot over an extended period of time. For the prospective mentor, The Broadcast Unit becomes that steady drop.

On the other hand, as long as there are clergy who lack a personal mentoring relationship, broadcast ministry is a means to hear the advice that is often times only heard behind the doors of privacy. As the listening audience tunes into the broadcast, they become exposed to the possibility of hearing answers to their own questions. Although the listening audience may participate by calling into the program, The Broadcast Unit will be limited by an absence of personal relationship. Many of the substantial qualities that make an apprenticeship valuable will not be available to the listening audience. The Broadcast Unit is not an ideal method of mentoring, but it does provide an alternative where nothing existed previously.

Once it is implemented, The Broadcast Unit will be a weekly talk forum where mentors serve as invited guests and share general wisdom concerning ministry and their experiences of being called, mentored and elevated into transformational leadership. The targeted audiences are men and women who do not have mentors, yet still need access to the wisdom that mentors are willing to share. Similar to the Conference Unit, the Broadcast Unit is a canvassing arena but it also raises the level of consciousness as it relates to mentoring.

The Mentoring Model is a living entity open to change and regular review. Although the model has been evaluated by a panel of clergy leaders, our research continues in the hopes of keeping the model relevant. For this reason a questionnaire is provided for your usage. The question before you at this point is whether or not you are open to the vision. Prayerfully the questionnaire will help you locate an honest answer to that question. We look forward to receiving your answers.

THE MENTORING MODEL SURVEY

PERSONAL DATA OF RESPONDENT
(Please circle your response)

1. Age of respondent.

    20-29   30-39   40-49   50-59   60-69   70+

2. What is your gender?

    Female   Male

3. Are you ordained?

    Yes   No

4. Number of years in ministry.

    1-5   6-10   11-16   17-22   23-28   29+

5. Number of years having served as a mentor.

    1-5   6-10   11-16   17-22   23-28   29+

6. Length of average mentoring relationship.

    6 months
    6mo - 1yr
    1 - 3yrs
    3 - 5yrs
    5 - 10yrs
    10+ yrs

7. Number of persons that you have mentored.

    1-5   6-10   11-16   17-22   23-28   29+

8. Have you been an apprentice to a clergyperson?

      Yes   No

9. How many clergy have mentored you.

      0   1-5   6-10   11-16   17-22 23-28 29+

10. Was your congregation involved in your mentoring experience?

      Yes   No

THE CLERGY MENTORING INSTITUTE™
(Intensive Training Unit)

1. How would you rate the one-year duration of the training unit?

   One year is too short 1   2   3   4   5   6   7 One year is too long

2. How would you rate the five-day frequency of the sessions?

   Five days is too short 1   2   3   4   5   6   7 Five days is too long

3. How would you rate the relevance of the weekly schedule for preparing mentors and apprentices for an intentional mentoring relationship?

   Not relevant at all 1   2   3   4   5   6   7 Very relevant

4. How important is it for a local congregation to be partners with the training unit?

   Not important at all 1   2   3   4   5   6   7 Very important

5. How meaningful for the local congregation would the partnership be?

   Not meaningful at all 1   2   3   4   5   6   7 Very meaningful

6. If a clergy person is reluctant about being a mentor, what is the probability that after participating in the training unit, they will become enthusiastic about being a mentor?

   Very low probability 1   2   3   4   5   6   7 Very high probability

7. How important is it for mentors and apprentices to participate jointly in the training unit?

   Not important at all 1   2   3   4   5   6   7 Very important

8. How willing do you think clergy will be to participate in the training unit?

   Not willing 1   2   3   4   5   6   7 Very willing

9. Average age of mentors who are likely to participate in mentor training?

   20-29   30-39   40-49   50-59   60-69   70+

10. Average age of apprentices who are likely to participate in mentor training?

    20-29   30-39   40-49   50-59   60-69   70+

11. After participating in the training unit, clergy will be better able to identify God's calling of leadership, upon the lives of other persons.

    No increase 1   2   3   4   5   6   7 Enormous increase

12. After participating in the training unit, clergy will implement intentional mentoring relationships with their ministerial staff members.

    Not likely 1   2   3   4   5   6   7 Very likely

13. After participating in the training unit, clergy will be better able to discern when it is time to elevate apprentices into leadership.

    No increase 1   2   3   4   5   6   7 Enormous increase

14. The training unit will persuade professional clergy to value the mentoring/apprentice process.

   Not likely 1   2   3   4   5   6   7 Very likely

15. Describe three ways the training unit will positively impact the Black church?

16. Describe three ways the training clinic will positively impact the Kingdom of God?

17. List two reasons why you would not participate in the training unit?

PROJECT PEER MENTORING
(The Peer Mentoring Unit)

18. How would you rate the bi-monthly frequency of the sessions?

   Too infrequent 1   2   3   4   5   6   7 Too frequent

19. How would you rate the 20-minute time allotment given to each ministry for discussion?

   Too short 1   2   3   4   5   6   7 Too long

20. How would you rate the structure of the unit?

   Too informal 1   2   3   4   5   6   7 Too formal

21. How important is it for spouses to be included?

   Not important at all 1   2   3   4   5   6   7 Very important

22. What is the ability of peers to mentor one another?

Very low ability 1   2   3   4   5   6   7 Very high ability

23. How important is it for clergy to mentor their peers?

Not important at all 1   2   3   4   5   6   7 Very important

24. Willingness of clergy to form peer-mentoring groups?

Not willing 1   2   3   4   5   6   7 Very willing

25. Average age of clergy who are likely to participate in peer mentoring?

20-29   30-39   40-49   50-59   60-69   70+

26. After participating in peer mentoring, clergy will be better able to identify God's calling of leadership, upon their peers.

No increase 1   2   3   4   5   6   7 Enormous increase

27. After participating in peer mentoring, clergy will implement intentional mentoring relationships with their ministerial staff members

Not likely 1   2   3   4   5   6   7 Very likely

28. Describe three ways that peer mentoring will impact those who participate?

29. List two reasons why you would not participate in peer mentoring?

THE CONFERENCE UNIT

30. Rate the willingness of churches, ministries and theological institutions that host leadership conferences to include clergy mentoring as a workshop.

Very low willingness 1   2   3   4   5   6   7 Very high willingness

31. Would the Conference Unit be valuable for attracting mentors?

Not likely 1   2   3   4   5   6   7 Very likely

32. Would the Conference Unit be valuable for attracting apprentices?

Not likely 1   2   3   4   5   6   7 Very likely

33. Would the Conference Unit be valuable for gaining congregational partnerships?

Not likely 1   2   3   4   5   6   7 Very likely

34. Rate the Conference Unit as an effective arena to canvass for clergy who would participate in the Intensive Training Unit (Clergy Mentoring Institute).

Not very effective 1   2   3   4   5   6   7 Very effective

THE BROADCAST UNIT

35. How would you rate the weekly frequency of the broadcast?

   Too infrequent 1   2   3   4   5   6   7 Too frequent

36. Would the Broadcast Unit be valuable for attracting mentors?

   Not likely 1   2   3   4   5   6   7   Very likely

37. Would the Broadcast Unit be valuable for attracting apprentices?

   Not likely 1   2   3   4   5   6   7   Very likely

38. Would the Broadcast Unit be valuable for gaining congregational partnerships?

   Not likely 1   2   3   4   5   6   7   Very likely

39. Rate the impact of the Broadcast Unit on laity.

   No impact 1   2   3   4   5   6   7 Enormous impact

40. Rate the impact of the Broadcast Unit on the clergy community.

   No impact 1   2   3   4   5   6   7   Enormous impact

41. Rate the Broadcast Unit as an effective arena to canvass for clergy to participate in the Intensive Training Unit (Clergy Mentoring Institute).

   Not very effective 1   2   3   4   5   6   7 Very effective

42. The Broadcast Unit will persuade professional clergy to value the mentoring/apprentice process.

   Not likely 1   2   3   4   5   6   7   Very likely

43. If a clergy person is reluctant about being a mentor, what is the probability that after listening to the Broadcast Unit over an extended period of time, they will become enthusiastic about being a mentor?

Very low probability 1   2   3   4   5   6   7 Very high probability

CHAPTER 10

"Say It GreeneBarr" —
A Sermon On Leadership

I have preached righteousness in the great congregation: lo, I have not refrained my lips, O LORD, thou knowest (Psalm 40:9 KJV).

Throughout this book I have presented biblical witness for the case of intentional leadership training. I have argued the case for redirecting existing ministerial agendas and reallocating personal and professional time in order to prepare new clergy leaders for the task of Kingdom leadership. I must admit that my approach up to this point has been clothed with logic alongside of a moderate amount of emotional layers. I depart this treatise after having laid aside the many thoughts that saturate the mind when time has been spent researching, and I leave you with the one thing that has always been able to carve out space in the human heart: a sermon.

I preached the sermon you are about to read at the Fourth Episcopal District Minister's Retreat of the African Methodist Episcopal Church. I was humbled when invited to bring a Word to this notable gathering of preachers and bishops. The sermon speaks to the leader inside all of us as we consider our actions through the eyes of those under our leadership. When the people look at us, do they want our leadership? With so much on the line, it is easy to see the value of having well prepared leaders.

Admittedly this is not an easy word to "SAY", but on this particular night God met us in the preaching moment and massaged the hearts of many. My prayer is that as you read the message, God will meet you at a meaningful point of intersection in your life as a leader. AMEN.

"A Leader Named Aaron"

Rev. Dr. Cecelia E. GreeneBarr

Then the anger of the Lord was as kindled against Moses and he said, "What of your brother Aaron the Levite? I know that he can speak fluently; even now he is coming out to meet you, and when he sees you his heart will be glad. You shall speak to him and put the words in his mouth; and I

*will be with your mouth and with his mouth, and
will teach you what you shall do. He indeed shall
speak for you to the people; he shall serve as a
mouth for you, and you shall serve as God for him
(Exodus 4:14-16).*

For several years now I've been giving myself over to
the study of biblical leadership. I've observed the leaders
that God placed in my life as instruments of instruction.
I've read scriptures, autobiographies, research papers, and
dissertations on the subject. I've interviewed successful and
not so successful leaders, productive and non-productive
leaders. I've talked to the Lord, my mentors, and my detractors
all for the purpose of enhancing my understanding of what
God seeks from those called into Kingdom leadership. I
wrestle with the topic all of the time so when one of my
leaders asked me, "What do you want in a leader?" I looked
to Aaron as a model to help formulate my response.

Why Aaron, because in Aaron I see not only the
origin of his calling but also the shifts and transitions of
his role, even to the end of his ministry and life. All at once
Aaron lived on a few planes of leadership, just like us. On
one level he has the Israelites who are his subordinates,
on another he has a quasi-lateral leadership with Moses,
and on another he has a superior, the Lord God Almighty. I
believe we all can identify with the particularity of Aaron's
role as a leader. The question is this; would I want Aaron to
be my leader? When I consider that scripture says that out
of God's anger with Moses, Aaron was lifted into leadership
I wonder if I would want Aaron to be my leader. When I
consider that scripture says, during the short period of 40

days while Moses was in God's presence getting instructions for the people, Aaron relented to the people's demands and lead them in idol worship, I wonder if I would want Aaron to be my leader. Considering how jealous Aaron became of Moses, would I want Aaron to be my leader? I submit that the answer is not cut and dry, that in order to arrive faithfully at an answer one needs to look at the dynamics of leadership, both from Aaron's experiences and God's expectations.

Let's start with that first level; pastor and congregation. The relationship between a leader and the people they lead can be like traveling down a dirt road. If comfort is important to you, then you'll travel slowly down a dirt road. Otherwise, rocks might start to fly and hit your windshield. If it's a dry sunny day you'll have to roll up your windows to keep from choking. If it's been raining then mud will mess up that "Armour All" shine on your tires. Yes, it is best to drive slowly on a dirt road because if you don't, the ride will be intensely bumpy, but if you do it will be less bumpy. Either way it's not a smooth ride. Aaron could tell every preacher of the gospel and spiritual leader on all levels whether you are a pastor, presiding elder, superintendent, or bishop that leading the people God has appointed to your hands is not a smooth ride.

It was not smooth nor fast trying to get God's people delivered. Four hundred years of bondage at the hands of the Egyptians when the process of deliverance begins the people complain. The Israelite supervisors complain against Moses and Aaron because Pharaoh required bricks without straw. The entire congregation complained against Moses and Aaron because their diet had changed and they feared starvation. They complained against Moses and Aaron after hearing the spies report because they feared death. They complained against Moses and Aaron because they couldn't stand the fact that Moses and Aaron walked in the authority God had placed upon them. When God judged their rebellion against leadership the congregation complained against Aaron and Moses. When they were thirsty they complained against Moses and Aaron. When they were hungry they complained against Moses and Aaron.

So if I were one of those complaining Israelites whom God had placed under Aaron's leadership, would I even want Aaron to be my leader? With all of this dissatisfaction with Aaron and all of this uncooperative attitude towards Aaron, and all of the suspicions about Aaron, and the lack of confidence in his ability, the complete disbelief in his vision, with their contrite selves, "I think I know better, I'm sure I can do better self", would I even want Aaron to be my leader?

I don't' think I should just dismiss Aaron because I can't catch his vision. It's not that cut and dry, so I think it would help if we consider some other factors when trying to decide what we want in a leader. Dealing with us Israelites meant that Aaron would hear more complaints than compliments. Being the leader of mentally and physically enslaved people meant rejection on multiple layers. No one wants to hear complaints all of the time. Few are the leaders whose temperament is unmoved by negative and difficult people. I dare say how much of that behavior many of us would accept before we start calling down God's wrath on God's people. But I can not ignore the fact that 90percent of the time when the Israelites complained, Aaron did not call them ungrateful, instead he and Moses prayed for God's mercy for their situation. So when I look at that I would have to say that in this situation I would want Aaron.

I would want Aaron because he prayed for the people when they feared the promise of their future. In my leader I would want Aaron's ability to pray for us in spite of the fact that we sometimes worked as hard as we could against his authority. I would want Aaron to be my leader because when we criticized his methods he interceded to God. Aaron could have watched God destroy us without saying a word but he prayed. We need leaders who are not sidetracked by our laziness. We need leaders who are not discouraged by our disagreeable conversation. In my leader I want Aaron's ability to forgive my ignorance. In my leader I want Aaron's ability to continue to lead even though I don't think we are going anywhere worthwhile. I may not want my leader to have all of Aaron's qualities but in these areas, I want Aaron when I see how he relates to his subordinates, but would I want Aaron to be my leader when I see how he relates to Moses?

What is God seeking from those called into Kingdom leadership when it comes to this second level; lateral or quasi-lateral? The relationship between one leader to another leader can be like traveling along an inner city street, which after a long and treacherous winter has deteriorated the structure of the road and now it is filled with unannounced potholes. Inner city driving is not like driving in the country where you can sort of relax your mind and take in the scenery. Inner city driving is compounded by the noise of car horns, lights to speed through before they turn red, people walking into the intersection and lots of potentially dangerous drivers for whom you must share the road. And yes, you must share the road which means one of your fellow drivers will need to merge in at a bottle neck. And you do expect to share those shifts in the traffic pattern but you don't expect the potholes, so when you hit one you usually do a lot of damage. Relationships on lateral and quasi-lateral levels; pastor to pastor, elder to elder, bishop to bishop are complicated, noisy, and as Aaron, Miriam and Moses experienced, it has unannounced potholes.

I know we don't like to put people into categories but the truth is Aaron was the number two man. The best thing for a leader to have is a really good number two man or woman. But the worse thing for a leader to have is a number two who thinks they can out do you at being number one. God warns us against comparing ourselves to other leaders because what we forget is that the harvest is plentiful and the laborers are few. We seem to forget that God gives gifts to each one as the Spirit wills. We seem to forget that we are all needed for the edifying of the body and the building up of the saints. We seem to forget that we all have this treasure in our earthen vessels for which is the Excellency of God in Christ Jesus (2Cor. 4:7). Aaron was busy being used of God and he was busy being in God's presence with Moses until he crossed a boundary between himself and his colleague.

Scripture tells us that Aaron and his sister Miriam became jealous of their brother, Moses. Yes, Aaron was the older brother. Yes, Aaron probably held some level of respect and authority while Moses was living outside of their closed community.

With so much ground to be won for God, why do God's leaders become jealous of one another? With thousands of people in every city walking around daily without ever hearing the gospel message, why are God's leaders jealous of one another? May I go out on a limb and ask if anyone in the room knows anything about jealousy among the ranks of God's leaders? Is it our system and the method of how one is promoted that creates the jealousy? That can't be the entire story because there is jealousy among Baptists, even though their system is different. There is also jealousy among non-denominational leaders. Jealousy exists between the young and the old. Jealousy exists among men and jealousy exists among women. No relationship is safe because Aaron and Miriam show us that jealousy even exists among siblings. And worse of all, we think no one sees this side of our sinful leadership. But the entire camp could not move forward for a period of seven days because they had to wait for Miriam to be cleansed from her sin.

When your destiny is being held up because of your leader's jealousy among his or her peers you might find yourselves asking the question, "Do I want Aaron to be my leader?" The Israelites were under authority of Aaron but as they watched their leader disrespect the anointing of God on others in authority they had to ask themselves, "Do I want Aaron to be my leader?" If Aaron can not accept that

God calls whom he wills, if he can't remember that God's favor rests upon those God chooses, if Aaron can't accept that Moses and God have a connection, if Aaron conspires behind Moses' back, if Aaron harbors hate towards Moses' position, then I don't want Aaron.

Give me someone who recognizes that we have not chosen God, but that God has chosen each of us. Give me someone who doesn't feel diminished just because their participation is on a different level. God requires his leaders to be on one accord before the power of the Holy Spirit can have full course in our ministries and lives. Aaron, you can be better than that. Aaron you can rise above pettiness. Aaron, we need you to be a leader who is comfortable in how God chooses to use him. Aaron, we need you to walk in your gifts; everybody agrees you are a good speaker, walk in your gift. Look at how the buds have sprouted on your rod, walk in your gifts.

This leadership thing is not so cut and dry. What do you want in your leader? And what happens when your leader has both of Aaron's strengths and Aaron's weaknesses? In other words, what happens when your leader is not hitting your standards of perfection? I've heard God say many times that our righteousness is as filthy rages (Isaiah 64:6). God says that all have sinned and come short of God's glory (Romans 3:23). We are all saved by grace, less none of us should boast (Ephesians 2:9). David was the apple of God's eye, but David did have Urriah killed. Joseph would be used to save his family, but he did speak too soon. Abraham was the father of many nations but he did lie about his relationship to Sarah. Sampson was a

Nazarite but he could not keep the secret of his strength from Delilah. Jeremiah was a strong voice for God, but he did suffer from depression. There has to be another criterion to weigh in when discerning the qualities of one fit for Kingdom leadership, and we find it on this last level; leader to creator.

The relationship between leader and creator is like the "road less traveled". Is it really that hard to finish well? Forty years in the wilderness, in the ministry, and you don't finish well enough to be able to enter into the kingdom? And what was the reason? Because he didn't trust in God and show God's holiness before the people! Scripture says that while the people were enjoying the refreshing water, God was announcing judgment upon the leader. The people's needs had been met but the leader had been judged by God for not trusting in Him. Is it really that hard to finish well? Is it so hard to finish well that God's people make it into the Kingdom but the leaders don't? I know we want God to cut Aaron some slack, because after all he was probably depressed, he had just buried his sister. Whether we are depressed, angry, disappointed, frustrated, confused or sleep deprived the answer is still the same – God shares his glory with no one. I don't believe Aaron was chosen for failure, but what happened to Aaron is probably what happens to so many other leaders.

The resources are few but the people's demands are high. The hours are long and rest is seldom peaceful. If this were simply a career you'd probably sign up with the union for more favorable working conditions. But it is not a career it is a calling. For one brief, emotionally depleted moment I think Aaron forgot that he had been called to this position by God. The Lord is seeking leaders who will at all times and under all conditions remember that this work that we do is not a career, it is a calling from the Lord. If it were just a career then faith would not be necessary. If it were just a career then prayer, study and meditation would not be necessary. If it were just a career then there would be no need to fast for direction. If it were just a career our degrees would suffice. If this thing called leadership were just a career then why stay where it seems you are not wanted nor appreciated? If it were just a career then the ends would justify the means. If it were just a career then all we would need are strategies instead of sanctification. Career people don't petition God, they just politic.

But the called know something that the career minded do not. The called have learned…

…how to wait on the Lord… how to be of good courage so that God can strengthen their hearts…that the effectual fervent prayers of the righteous availath much …that God will meet your need according to his riches in glory by Christ Jesus… not to fret because of evil doers for in a little while they will be no more … not to walk in the counsel of the ungodly… that God will perfect that which concernth them … that in God we live, move and have our being … that as for God, his way is perfect; the word of the Lord is tried; he is a buckler to all those that trust in him …the LORD *is* my light and my salvation; whom shall I fear? The LORD *is* the strength of my life; of whom shall I be afraid? …know their serving is not in vain …know they serve as unto to the Lord and not unto men …know that whatsoever good thing any man doeth, the same shall he receive of the Lord

…know how to press toward the mark for the prize of the high calling of God in Christ Jesus …the steps of a good man (woman) are ordered by the Lord, and he delighteth in his way… who shall separate the called from the love of Christ? *shall* tribulation, or distress, or persecution, or famine, or nakedness, or peril, or sword? …For the called are persuaded, that neither death, nor life, nor angels, nor principalities, nor powers, nor things present, nor things to come, nor height, nor depth, nor any other creature, shall be able to separate us from the love of God, which is in Christ Jesus our Lord.

To the leaders in the house tonight, you may have Aaron's strengths or you may have Aaron's weaknesses but for this season God has chosen you to do His will. Live as one called by God. Live in a manner that allows you and those under you to finish well. Live as one chosen by God. Leaders will have ups and downs but live a balanced life before the Lord. Live a consecrated life for God. Live like the leader that God destined you to be.

ABOUT THE AUTHOR

Rev. Dr. Cecelia E. GreeneBarr personally received God's plan of salvation more than 29 years ago through the confession of her sins and expressed belief that Jesus is the Son of God. She is a spirit filled citizen in the Kingdom of God who embraces the manifested gifts of the Holy Spirit. She has served as a minister of the gospel of Jesus Christ since preaching her initial sermon on June 13th 1993.

Her methodology and philosophy of ministry was molded by the effective tutelage of the late Rev. Dr. Samuel D. Proctor. Raised in the Baptist church, she is an Itinerant Elder in the African Methodist Episcopal Church - presently serving in the Fourth District - Michigan Annual Conference as the pastor of Trinity A. M. E. Church in Detroit. Prior to her appointment as the pastor of Trinity, she served as the Chief of Staff at St. Stephen A. M. E. Church in Chicago, IL where Rev. Albert D. Tyson, III is the pastor. During her tenure in ministry she has affected the body of Christ through the gifts of preaching, administration, diligence, and biblical instruction for Christian maturity.

Ministry beyond the congregation is realized as a member of the Michigan Annual Conference Board of Examiners, for which she serves as the Chair of First Year Studies. Dr. GreeneBarr works with other clergy through her involvement in the A. M. E. Ministerial Alliance of Southeastern Michigan, where she has served as the Secretary and Assistant

Secretary. Ecumenical involvement is actively achieved through such venues as the Pastors of Excellence Program that is administered by the Sandberg Leadership Center and funded by the Lily Foundation. Dr. GreeneBarr has been published in This is My Story: Testimonies and Sermons of Black Women in Ministry, The African American Pulpit (Summer 2005), and When Pastors Pray: The Prayers and Psalms of Pastors.

Involved in the community, she has served as a volunteer for Big Sisters of the Washington Metropolitan Area. Rev. Dr. GreeneBarr is also a life member of Delta Sigma Theta Sorority, Inc. a public service organization dedicated to Sisterhood, Scholarship and Service. She served four years as the Midwest Regional Chaplain. During her tenure as Chaplain she conducted workshops during Regional Conferences that were created specifically for chapter chaplains; she often preached the gospel message at Delta prayer breakfasts and Founder's Days as well as convened Regional Revivals.

In 1999, Rev. Dr. GreeneBarr contributed to the Kingdom of God through the founding of Sharing Faith Ministries, Inc. a Kingdom based ministry that promotes spiritual maturity. To this end, she conducts religious and educational services, activities and projects to spiritually assess and develop central personality competencies of motives, traits and self-identity consistent with the biblical mandate to take on the mind of Christ.

Rev. Dr. GreeneBarr submits to the work of ministry as a prepared servant. She is an honors graduate of North Carolina Agricultural and Technical State University with a Bachelor of Science degree in Industrial Technology in Manufacturing. She has gained additional training in Early Childhood Education from the University of the District of Columbia. Her theological education was completed at Princeton Theological Seminary where she earned a Master of Divinity degree and Ashland Theological Seminary where she earned a Doctor of Ministry degree in the area of Transformational Leadership with emphasis on Clergy Mentoring.

Dr. GreeneBarr and her husband Theron E. Barr, Jr. are the parents of two children; Theron-Howard and Cecelia.

SOURCES CITED

Alimo-Metcalfe, Beverly and Alban-Metcalfe, Robert J., 2001. *The Development of a New Transformational Leadership Questionnaire. Journal of Occupational and Organizational Psychology.* 09631798: Vol. 74, Issue 1 [journal online]; available from *Academic Search Premier,* www.EBSCOhost.edu (accessed August 2, 2002).

Abshire, David M. May 1, 2001. *A Call for Transformational Leadership. Vital Speeches of the Day.* 0042742X, Vol. 67, Issue 14. [journal online]; Available from Academic Search Premier, www.EBSCOhost.edu (accessed August 4,2002).

Anderson, Keith R. and Reese, Randy D.. 1999. *Spiritual Mentoring: A Guide for Seeking and Giving Direction.* Downers Grove, IL.: InterVarsity Press.

Barna Research. January 7, 2002. *Pastors Rate Themselves Highly, Especially As Teachers.* [online] Available from www.barna. org/cgi-bin/PagePressRelease.asp?PressReleaseID=104& Reference=B. Internet; (accessed January 11, 2002).

_____. July 2, 2002. *Christian Mass Media Reach More Adults With the Christian Message Than Do Churches.* [online] Available from www.barna.org/cgi-bin/PagePressRelease.asp ?PressReleaseID=116&Reference=A. Internet; (accessed July 27, 2002).

Berlinger, Lisa. 2000. *Competencies for Leadership. Private publication. Distributed in class. August 2000.*

Cannistraci, David. *Apostles and the Emerging Apostolic Movement: A Biblical Look at Apostleship And How God Is Using It To Bless His Church Today.* Ventura, CA., Renew Books.

Carson, Felisha. 2002. "A Seminarian Speaks: A Call For Mentors." *The African American Pulpit.* Vol. 5. No. 3. (Summer): pp. 9-11.

Clinton, J. Robert. 1988. *The Making of a Leader.* Colorado Springs, CO: Navpress.

Copeland, Claudette. 1998. *On The Way To Purpose.* Sermon preached at the Ebenezer AMEC 14th Annual Women's Spiritual Retreat. Ft. Washington, Md.: Ebenezer AMEC Multimedia Production. Videocassette #S166.

Corporate Mentoring Solutions, Inc. *Mentoring vs. Coaching?* [online] Available from www.mentoring.ws.products/ mentoring_vs_coaching.asp?i=5. Internet; (accessed July 31, 2002).

Dean, Ben. "Coaching vs. Therapy." *Current Thoughts & Trends.* (February 2002): p. 14.

Driscoll, Mark. 2000. "Generation to Generation." *Leadership.* 21 (Spring): p. 40.

Evans, James H., 1992. *We Have Been Believers: An African American Systematic Theology. Minneapolis, MN.: Fortress Press.*

Galbraith, Michael W. and Norman H. Cohen. *Issues and Challenges Confronting Mentoring. New Directions for Adult Continuing Education.* 66 (Summer 1995): pp. 90-91.

Gibson, Eugene. 2002. "To Be Or Not To Be: That Is The Question." *The African American Pulpit.* (Winter 2001-2002): pp. 10-13.

Gill, Jeffery A. *The Value of Coupling Mentor-Protégé Relationships with Persuasive Messages About Relational Evangelism to Increase Involvement in Relational Evangelism. Doctorate of Ministry dissertation, Denver* Conservative Baptist Seminary, 1997.

Goleman, Daniel. 1998.Working with Emotional Intelligence. New York: Bantam Books.

Grudem, Wayne. 1994. *Systematic Theology.* Grand Rapids, MI.: Zondervan.

Grundstein-Amado and Rivka. May 1999. *Bilateral Transformational Leadership, Administration and Society,* 00953997 Vol. 31, Issue 2. [journal online]. Available from Academic Search Premier, www.EBSCOhost.edu. Internet; (accessed August 4, 2002).

Healy, Charles C. and Alice J. Welchart 1990. "Mentoring Relations: A Definition to Advance Research and Practice." *Educational Researcher.* 19: 17.

Hendricks, Howard. and William. 1995. *As Iron Sharpens Iron: Building Character In A Mentoring Relationship.* Chicago: Moody Press.

Herrington, Jim, Bonem, Mike and James H. Furr. 2000. *Leading Congregational Change.* San Francisco: Jossey-Bass.

Jacobs, Cindy. 1995. *The Voice of God.* Ventura, CA.: Regal Books.

Jason, Martin H., Feb/Mar2000. "The Role of the Principal as Transformational Leader in a Multicultural Learning Community" (N1). *High School Journal,* 00181498, Vol. 83, Issue 3. [journal online]. Available from Academic Search Premier www.EBSCOhost.edu. Internet; (accessed August 4, 2002).

Kinnon, Joy Bennett. 1997. "15 Greatest Black Women Preachers." *Ebony Magazine.* (November): pp. 102-114.

Lincoln, Eric C. and Lawrence H. Mamiya 1990. *The Black Church in the African American Experience.* Durham and London: Duke Press.

Mahlangu-Ngcobo, Mankekolo. 1992. *The Preaching of Bishop John Bryant.* Baltimore, MD.: Victory Press.

Malphurs, Aubrey, interviewed by Cecelia Greene Barr, telephone tape recording, Dallas, TX. March 29, 2002.

McFarland, Randy. 2001. *Mentoring That Changes Lives.* [online]. Available from www.Forministry.com/qryArticlePrint. asp?Record=1455. Internet; (accessed June 1, 2001).

_____. Interviewed by Cecelia Greene Barr, telephone tape recording, Denver, CO. June 20, 2002.

McKenzie, Vashti M. 2000. African Methodist Episcopal Church General Conference.

McNeal, Reggie. 2000. *A Work of Heart: Understanding How God Shapes Spiritual Leaders.* San Francisco, CA.: Jossey-Bass.

Miami Mass Choir. 2001. *What God Has For Me.* James Virginia - Cleveland: Savoy Gospel Classics.

Migliore, Daniel L., 1991. *Faith Seeking Understanding: An Introduction to Christian Theology.* Grand Rapids, MI: Eerdmans.

Milavec, Aaron. 1982. *To Empower As Jesus Did: Acquiring Spiritual Power Through Apprenticeship.* Lewiston, NY: The Edwin Mellen Press.

Miller, Patrick D. Jr. "Toward A Theology of Leadership: Some Clues From The Prophets." *The Asbury Theological Journal.* Vol. 47. No. 1 (Spring 1992): pp. 43-50.

_____. Interviewed by Cecelia Greene Barr, telephone tape recording, Princeton, NJ. April 1, 2002.

Moots, Paul A. 1999. "Son of Encouragement." *The Christian Ministry.* (July-August): pp. 22-25.

Munroe, Myles. 1991. *Understanding Your Potential.* Shippensburg, PA.: Destiny Image Publishers.

Murray, Margo and Owen, Marna A. 1991. *Beyond the Myths and Magic of Mentoring.* San Francisco: Jossey-Bass Publishers.

Myers, William H. 1992. *The Irresistible Urge To Preach: A Collection of African American "Call" Stories.* Atlanta, GA.: Aaron Press.

Nash, Diane and Don Treffinger 1991. *The Mentor.* Melbourne: Hawker Brownlow Education.

Nore'n, Carol M. 1992. *The Woman In The Pulpit.* Nashville: Abington Press.

Oden, Thomas C. 1983. *Pastoral Theology: Essentials of Ministry.* New York: HarperSanFrancisco.

Payne, Don. A Theology of Mentoring. Cassette. The National Conference on Mentoring: Denver Seminary. April 12, 2002.

Proctor, Samuel D. 1989. *My Moral Odyssey. Valley Forge: Judson Press.*

Schnase, Robert. *1993. Ambition in Ministry: Our Struggle with Success, Achievement & Competition.* Nashville: Abingdon Press.

Spencer Institute. *About Coaching.* [online]. Available from www.spencerinstitute.com/aboutcoaching.html. Internet; (accessed July 31, 2002).

Sweetman, John Raymond. *The Assessment of a Self-Study Course Designed to Develop Mentoring Commitment and Competency Among Australian Baptist Church Leaders. D.Min. dissertation, Denver Conservative Baptist Seminary. 1999.*

"The 15 Greatest Black Preachers." Ebony Magazine; Nov 1993, v49n1. p.156-168.

Thurman, Howard. *1979. With Head and Heart: The Autobiography of Howard Thurman.* San Diego, New York: Harcourt Brace Jovanovich.

Trofino, A.J., Dec. 2000. "Transformational Leadership: Moving Total Quality Management to World-Class Organizations." *International Nursing Review,* 00208132, Vol. 47, Issue 4 [journal online] Available from Academic Search Premier, www.EBSCOHost.edu. Internet; (accessed August 5, 2002).

Webster's II: New Riverside University Dictionary. 1984. Riverside Publishing Co.

West, Cornel. 1998. *Prophetic Fragments: Illuminations of the Crisis in American Religion and Culture.* Grand Rapids, MI: Eerdmans and Trenton, N.J.: Africa World Press, Inc.

Westing, Harold, Sr. interviewed by Cecelia Greene Barr, telephone tape recording, Denver, CO. June 10, 2002.

Williams, Walton A. *The Impact of Mentor Training on Seventh-Day Adventist Senior Pastors and Interns Participating In A Formal Mentoring Program. D.Min. dissertation, Denver Seminary, 2001.*

_____. Interviewed by Cecelia Greene Barr, telephone conversation, June 10, 2002, Tennessee.

Yusof, Aminuddin. Early Winter 1998. "The Relationship Between Transformational Leadership Behaviors of Athletic Directors and Coaches' Job Satisfaction." *Physical Educator,* 00318981, Vol. 55, Issue 4. [journal online] Available from Academic Search Premier www.EBSCOhost.edu. Internet; (accessed August 4, 2002).

ADDITIONAL BIBLIOGRAPHY

Agosto, Efrain. "The Apostle Paul & Mentoring: Formal & Informal Approaches." Apuntes. 18: No. 1 (Spring 1998). pp. 10-13.

Bilezikian, Gilbert. 2000. "It's a Natural Process." *Leadership.* 21 (Spring): 40.

Bridges, William. 1991. *Managing Transitions.* Cambridge, MA: Perseus Books.

Cerbone, Mark. September-October 1996. "Come, Follow Me." *Sojourner* [journal online]; Available from www.sojo. net/9609/article960941d.html. Internet; (accessed January 12, 2002).

Clayton, Paul C. 1999. *Letters to Lee: Mentoring the New Minister.* The Alban Institute.

Houston, James M. 2002. *The Mentored Life.* Colorado Springs, CO: Navpress.

Johnson, Erik. 2000. "How To Be An Effective Mentor." *Leadership. 21 (Spring): pp. 36-42.*

Jones, Timothy K. 1991. "Believer's Apprentice." *Christianity Today.* 35. (March 11 1991): pp. 42-44.

Klassen, Michael. 2001. *The Art of Mentoring: An Interview with Dr. Howard Hendricks.* [on-line] Available from www.fm2. forministry.com/qryArticlePrint.asp?Record=1813; Internet; (accessed June 8, 2002).

_____. 2001. *How To Build An Effective Mentoring Ministry In Your Church.* [online]. Available from www.fm2.forministry. com/qryArticlePrint.asp?Record=2021; Internet; (accessed June 8, 2002).

Lightner, Ann Farrar. 1995. *And Your Daughters Shall Preach: Developing a Female Mentoring Program in the African American Church.* St. Louis, MO: Hodale Press, Inc.

Marty, Martin E. 1995. Pastors Attract Pastors. The Christian Century.112. N27. (September 27, 1995): 911.

McCarty, Doran. 1983. *The Supervision of Ministry Students.* Atlanta: Home Mission Board, SBC.

McKenzie, Vashti M. 1996. *Not Without a Struggle: Leadership Development for African American Women in Ministry.* Cleveland, OH: United Church Press.

Myers, William H. 1994. *God's Yes Was Louder Than My No: Rethinking the African-American Call to Ministry.* Grand Rapids, MI and Trenton, NJ: William B. Eerdmans Publishing Company and Africa World Press.

Nance, Terry. 1994. *God's Armorbearer II.* Tulsa, OK: Harrison House.

Northouse, Peter G. 2001. *Leadership: Theory and Practice.* Second edition. Thousand Oaks, CA: Sage Publications.

Pohly, Kenneth. 1993. *Transforming The Rough Places: The Ministry of Supervision.* Dayton, OH; Whaleprints.

Proctor, Samuel D. and Gardner C. Taylor. 1996. *We Have This Ministry: The Heart of the Pastor's Vocation.* Valley Forge: Judson Press.

Roberts, Bob Jr., Fred Smith, Charles R Swindoll. "Training with a Championship Coach: Finding a Mentor can Help with your Ministry." *Leadership. 17 (Summer 1996): pp. 54, 56-59.*

Simmons, Charitey. Leaders for Black Churches *Christian Century*, 2/1/95, Vol. 112, Issue 4, p. 100, 3 p. [online]. Available from www.EBSCOhost.edu. Internet; (accessed July 31, 2002).

Woolfe, Lorin. 2002. *The Bible On Leadership: From Moses to Matthew — Management Lessons for Contemporary Leaders.* New York:AMACOM — American Management Association.

Religious Services
Educational Seminars
Leadership Projects

The Clergy Mentoring Institute™

Mail your questionnaire to:

Sharing Faith Ministries
P.O. Box 3746
Southfield, Michigan 48037

www.sharing-faith.org
mentor@sharing-faith.org

Other Resources *by* Cecelia E. GreeneBarr

ORDER FORM

VHS	PRICE	QTY	AMOUNT
About My Father's Business	$10		
CD			
Discouragement Will Not Get the Best of Me	$10		
My Reasons for Outward Praise	$10		
When the Gates are Opened	$10		
Your Actions Caused Me to Need a Miracle	$10		
Quarantined by Spiritual Gifts	$10		
DVD			
Riding in On Destiny	$15		
TOTAL *(Please add $3 each item for shipping and handling)*			

Please print:

Name_____

Address_____

City_____State_____Zip_____

Phone_____

Email_____

MAIL ORDER FORM TO:
GreeneHouse, LLC • P.O. Box 714, Walled Lake, MI 48390
Make checks payable to GreeneHouse, LLC
Expect orders within 2-3 weeks

Visit www.greenehousellc.com for new sermon releases and other products

greenehouse LLC

Come Where Vision Grows™

To schedule **Rev. Dr. Cecelia GreeneBarr**
for speaking engagements or to order
additional copies of this book,
Call — 248.980.8050,
Email — sales@greenehousellc.com,
Write — GreeneHouse, LLC
P.O. Box 714
Walled Lake, Michigan 48390-0714
Or visit her online at
www.greenehousellc.com